Goodbye Canada

Feb. 19, 2002

To: Doug Martin

with my best wish

Paul T. Hellyer

PAUL T. HELLYER

Chimo Media

Canadian Cataloguing in Publication Data

Hellyer, Paul, 1923-
  Goodbye Canada

Includes bibliographical references and index.
ISBN 0-9694394-8-2

1. Canada – Economic Policy – 1991. 2. Globalization. 3.
  Free Trade. 4. Canada-Annexation to the United States.

HC115.H462 2001-07-20   338.971   C2001-902192-5

Printed and bound in Canada. The paper used in this book is acid free.

Chimo Media Inc.
99 Atlantic Ave., Suite 302
Toronto, ON M6K 3J8
Canada
Tel: (416) 535-0514
Fax: (416) 535-6325

ACKNOWLEDGMENTS

A number of individuals have been especially helpful in the preparation of this book. I am indebted to Fred Brown, Stephen Burega, Catherine Hellyer, Peter Hellyer, Jim Jordan and Mike McCracken for reading the draft manuscript. Their insightful comments and suggestions were of immense value in preparing the final version. They also noted a number of errors and omissions. Responsibility for those that slipped through the net, and for the views expressed, is mine alone.

Once again Andy Donato has managed to capture the reality of the situation in his cartoon for the cover. It is a sad picture, but then seeing one's country go down the drain is hardly an occasion for rejoicing.

I am grateful to those who helped dig out the facts and figures to support my thesis. David Banerjee, Stephen Burega, Wendy Lamb and Veera Pavri all spent endless hours either at the Metropolitan Toronto Reference Library, or checking books and documents and surfing the internet in search of information.

My thanks to Christopher Blackburn for preparing the index in such a professional manner. He earned extra points for noting a number of errors in need of correction.

As always, my executive assistant, Nina Moskaliuk, deserves special mention. Once again, she was painstaking in her research and verification of references, as well as indefatigable in revising the text and preparing the pages for the printer.

Finally, I have to thank my wife, Ellen, one more time. She is the one who has paid the price for my preoccupation with national affairs. I only hope that if Canada is saved, and our grandchildren are blessed with the same choice that we had, she will be able to look back and believe that it was all worthwhile.

Other Books by the Same Author

Agenda: A Plan for Action (1971)

Exit Inflation (1981)

Jobs For All: Capitalism on Trial (1984)

Canada at the Crossroads (1990)

Damn the Torpedoes (1990)

Funny Money:
A Common Sense Alternative to Mainline Economics (1994)

Surviving the Global Financial Crisis:
The Economics of Hope for Generation X (1996)

Arundel Lodge: A Little Bit of Old Muskoka (1996)

The Evil Empire: Globalization's Darker Side (1997)

Stop: Think (1999)

CONTENTS

INTRODUCTION

When I knocked on doors during the federal election of November, 2000, I would say to the person who answered "my name is Paul Hellyer, and the only reason I am running in this election is because I think we are losing our country." I would then go on to provide a few facts and figures to support my statement. If the voter appeared interested, and not too rushed, I would sometimes add that I thought we were losing our democracy, as well, and provide a few examples of where we have already lost it.

About one person out of every ten knew exactly what I was talking about. The others, the vast majority, were absolutely oblivious to what is going on in Canada and the world. Usually they were speechless, although quite willing to accept the flyer I handed them. Sometimes there was a little nervous giggle of disbelief – a shock reaction similar to the one that sometimes occurs when someone is told there has been an accident, and a loved one has been killed. There is instant denial until the police and coroner arrive at the door and the truth becomes all too tragically evident.

Occasionally I would get the following reaction. I was told that globalization was inevitable and, by inference, good; that national boundaries are obsolete; that this is the wave of the future and that I might just as well "get with it". There was no point in arguing because there was nothing to argue about. Globalization is a *fait accompli* and anyone who doesn't realize that is stuck in some kind of time warp.

I freely admit that globalization is the essence of my concern and it begins with the meaning of the word itself. It has become a kind of a catch-all for everything that is going on in the world. Rarely do you see any distinction being made between those aspects of globalization which are good and those that are not; between what is inevitable and what is not.

This lack of distinction was underlined for me by a conference held at the University of Toronto, March 8-10, 2001. The name "Reinventing Society in a Changing Global Economy" gave the game away. An unfettered global economy was taken as a given. Several of the speakers said they didn't like the idea, but none challenged its inevitability. The only ray of hope in this sea of despair was John Ralston Saul, in his keynote address, when he said "nothing is inevitable." No doubt he was excluding death and taxes, but this doesn't detract from his welcome proclamation of hope and optimism.

My guarded optimism begins with a more precise use of words. In the search for a better way to explain globalization I thought of cholesterol. There is good cholesterol and bad cholesterol. One is life enhancing, and the other can kill you. It is the same with globalization. The good globalization is technologically driven. The internet is a good example. It is opening up access to a range of knowledge almost beyond imagination. So apart from the risk of addiction and a few other problem areas, the net benefit is very positive.

The bad globalization is the relentless drive on the part of the richest, most powerful people in the world to re-engineer the global economy for their own benefit. This most alarming aspect of globalization is agenda driven. For decades, a relatively small group of people have persistently and methodically paved the way for a single, seamless world economy beneficial to them.

In the process they are perverting the word democracy. It no longer means government of, by and for the people. That is part of the plan. They are in the process of substituting a kind of elite global governance as an alternative to the power of nation states. They cutely refer to the results as a "democracy deficit" because it is easier to sell, and it sounds less alarming than to tell the truth, i.e. that this is the end of our 200 year experiment in popular democracy.

The globalizers are succeeding by using a clever mixture of "fog" and "grease". The fog has been the brain-washing to which we have been subjected. Week after week, we are bombarded by columns and editorials which refer to "the unquestioned benefits of globalization." Sometimes the writers admit that there is a problem with the distribution of benefits but present this as a minor irritant without suggesting what can be done about it. Never have I seen any complete and honest data to back the claim of "global benefits".

The reason is clear. The data for the last 25 years, since the global concept really caught fire, shows clearly that this experiment has been a disaster. Once or twice when economists try to support their case with statistics, they go back 50 years to include the superior performance of the Keynesian era.

This is highly misleading as is the entire effort to prove that black is white. The constant use of "the un-questioned benefits of globalization," without evidence in support, is a blatant example of "tell a lie big enough and often enough, and people will believe it." The near universal acceptance of globalization as being both inevitable and good for mankind is the worst case of brain-washing since the Third Reich in the 1930s.

The "grease" side of the operation has been the increasing ability of the globalizers to "buy" governments which willingly hand over the sovereignty of their people to unelected, unaccountable bureaucrats. To say that these governments were elected "democratically" is to give a whole new meaning to the word.

To be a little bit kind to the politicians one senses that they may be blissfully unaware of the extent to which they are being manipulated. When U.K. Prime Minister Tony Blair visited Ottawa on February 22, 2001, en route to Washington, and spoke out on behalf of global free trade, I was convinced that he was a victim of the people who wrote his notes. Still the buck has to stop somewhere, and he certainly had not earned the award for bravery he subsequently received from the *Globe and Mail*.

The globalizers have also twisted the word reform. When former U.S. President Bill Clinton or Canadian Finance Minister Paul Martin use the word in the context of Third World countries, it really means "capitulate" or "surrender". It means that they must change their economic systems – in order to get loans or debt relief – to accommodate the demands of international big business even though the "reforms" will ultimately hurt them more than help them.

So these are some of the issues that I will address in this book. I would like readers to have a better understanding of why thoughtful people would risk so much to demonstrate against the World Trade Organization and the Free Trade Area of the Americas. I would like them to understand that the words "free trade", too, do not mean what they say.

"Free trade" and "globalization" are really code words for "corporate rule" and "colonization". And in Canada's case, due to our unique geographical position vis-à-vis the United States, first colonization and then annexation. The new world without borders will be like a zoo without cages. Only the most powerful of the species will survive. Canada will not be one of them.

This book is really to sound the alarm which could lead to the revolution of the intellect and then the revolution of the ballot box, essential for survival. Time is short, so I will use as few words as possible in making the case even at the expense of omitting the occasional caveat which might be helpful in a longer treatise.

I will content myself with making the case for a continued important role for the nation state; against unrestricted global investment; against the substitution of a feudal system and elite rule for democracy; for a better distribution of income worldwide and a more just society everywhere; and why, in my opinion, Canada is worth saving. Then it can shed its current mediocrity and become, once again, a progressive and dynamic middle power playing its own, independent role on the world stage while proving that people of different race, language and religion can work together in harmony for the betterment of all.

Readers familiar with my work will note that some of the arguments have been borrowed from earlier books, and there will be a certain amount of repetition. This is not inadvertent. Some of the principal points need to be emphasized over and over again.

Finally, it must be admitted that I am of a generation unschooled in the niceties of political correctness and inclusive language. I hope that I may be forgiven for expressing my hopes and concerns without fear or favour.

CHAPTER 1

GOODBYE CANADA

*"The Canadians don't understand what they have signed.
In 20 years they will be sucked into the U.S. economy."*

Clayton Yeutter[1]

This statement, blurted out by the chief U.S. trade
negotiator the day the Canada-United States Free Trade
Agreement (FTA) was signed, has been studiously ignored by
Canadians even though it should have sounded a warning
bell. Yeutter inadvertently telegraphed the end result of the
new relationship which will be the death of Canada and the
birth of the 51st U.S. state.

Canadians were duped into believing that the FTA
was a trade agreement. I was naïve enough to believe it
because that is what I heard on television and radio and what
I read in the newspapers. Most Canadians still believe that
"Free Trade" means free trade. But it doesn't! It is much
more complicated than that. Anyone who has actually read
either the FTA, or its successor agreement the North
American Free Trade Agreement (NAFTA), as I eventually
did, will know that these treaties are primarily about
investment, and corporate rights.

Of course the FTA eliminated tariffs between the two
countries over a ten-year period but these were already
coming off under the General Agreement on Tariffs and
Trade (GATT). So by the time the FTA was signed most
items were already duty free and for those items where tariffs
still applied, Canada had an advantage because our tariffs

were higher than those in the U.S. – an advantage that we gave up.

From the outset the two countries had very different objectives. These were stated during an initial meeting of Prime Minister Brian Mulroney's Chief of Staff, Derek Burney, and Senior Deputy United States Trade Representative, Michael B. Smith, on July 31, 1985.

Canadians wanted just two things: "Exemption from the application of U.S. Dumping and Anti-Subsidy laws, and a gradual phase-in, indeed a back-end loading, of tariff eliminations." The U.S. had two demands: "Immediate abolition of the infamous Foreign Investment Review Board (FIRB) and a faster implementation of Canadian tariff reductions, given the fact that Canadian tariffs were already higher than U.S. tariffs."[2]

In the end the Americans achieved both of their demands and Canada struck out on its two bottom-line objectives. We did not get an exemption from U.S. anti-dumping and countervailing duty laws which can be applied almost capriciously whenever the American political situation demands.

Also, Canada did not gain "guaranteed access" to U.S. markets, as we were told we would. Just ask the cement manufacturers, steel producers or softwood lumber producers. But the Americans did get their "license" to buy Canada, and that is exactly what they are doing – for 65 cents on the dollar.

From June 30, 1985, to June 30, 2001, almost 13,000 Canadian companies have been sold to foreigners[3] – the vast majority to our cousins south of the border. This figure only includes transactions subject to the Investment Canada Act. Furthermore, the dollar value of companies sold in 1999 was double that of 1998, which was itself a record. "You've got to be concerned that you're losing control of your own destiny," said Ian Macdonell, a partner at Crosbie & Company Inc., a Toronto investment banking firm which tracks mergers and acquisitions.[4]

A few of the better known companies sold include Aikenhead Hardware, acquired by Home Depot; Canstar, with its world famous Bauer line of sports equipment, by

Nike; Club Monaco Inc., by Polo Ralph Lauren Inc.; Le Groupe Forex by Louisiana Pacific; MacMillan Bloedel, the icon of British Columbia's forest industry, by Weyerhaeuser; Midland Walwyn, Canada's last remaining large independent broker, by New York-based Merrill Lynch; the Montreal Canadiens hockey team by George N. Gillette, Jr., Shoppers Drug Mart by New York-based Kohlberg Kravis & Roberts Co.; St. Laurent Paperboard Inc. by Smurfit-Stone Container Corp., North America's biggest packaging group; Tim Hortons by Wendy's; Trentway Wager bus to Coach USA; and just as this paragraph was being written, Gulf Canada Resources Ltd. was acquired by Houston-based Conoco, in the largest corporate take-over in Canadian oil and gas history. It will not be the last, and the deal proves that even the largest Canadian corporations are not immune.

The list goes on and on and the end is not in sight. It would take almost two books the size of this one to list, line by line, the companies already sold. Still, in March 2000, John Manley, then the Minister of Trade and Commerce, and a potential candidate for the Liberal leadership, in an interview with the *National Post* predicted the end of federal restrictions that limit foreign ownership of Canadian airlines, communications companies and even banks. "It is coming down the road," he said in a stunning admission from a senior minister in a Liberal government that pretends to care about Canadian sovereignty.[5]

You don't have to be a rocket scientist to know that it is only a matter of time before companies like Shaw and Rogers cable will be taken over by American conglomerates, Air Canada will be bought by an American carrier, Bell Canada with CTV in tow will be bought, probably by AT&T, and all of the banks will be either owned or controlled by international banks of the scale of J.P. Morgan Chase or Citigroup Inc., and it won't make any difference whether the Canadian banks are merged or not.

Most recently Canadian Pacific announced that it is splitting into five separate companies in order to maximize shareholder values. Apart from the dubious proposition that there are no stakeholders other than shareholders, which will be addressed later in this book, the writing on the wall foreshadows the sale of the Canadian Pacific Railway (CPR) to an American company.

It hardly seems possible that the band of steel that bound Canada together as a country is about to go on the auction block. This is sacrilege and the government must stiffen its spine and say "no", "absolutely not". It is bad enough that the Canadian National Railway (CNR) is now majority owned by Americans without letting the historic CPR slip out of our hands.

Apologists for the FTA say: "Yes, some Canadian companies are being bought by Americans but Canadians are buying U.S. companies as well." That is true. Canadians, as well as foreign-owned Canadian companies, have been buying them in large numbers and this heavy foreign investment is one of the most important reasons the Canadian dollar is so low.

The bottom line, however, is that there is not one major industry in the U.S. dominated by Canadians. In Canada, however, our automobile, gasoline, tire, chemical, soft drinks and many other industries are completely dominated by foreigners. And it is only a matter of time until transportation, telecommunications and banking are added to the list.

NOTHING IS SACRED

I was at first incredulous when I learned that Laura Secord chocolates had been sold to Americans. Laura had been a symbol of Canadian sovereignty. Her picture on the cover of some of our favourite bon bons reminded us of her bravery in leading her cow through the American lines to warn General Isaac Brock of an imminent attack. This selfless act on her part played a significant role in helping us to win that war. Now we are losing this one without a single shot being fired.

With the FTA, Brian Mulroney accomplished two things. He virtually guaranteed the demise of Canada as a nation state; and he allowed Ronald Reagan to accomplish with one stroke of the pen what American generals and

American armies had been unsuccessful in doing on more than one occasion – to conquer Canada.

The secret weapon that is making this possible is the "national treatment" clause, which the Americans insisted be incorporated in the treaty. Despite its critical importance in international investment law approximately 98% of Canadians don't know about it. It gives foreign investors the same rights in the host country as citizens of that country. In theory it is reciprocal, but in practice the advantage accrues to the big guns and allows them to silence the little ones.

In my opinion "national treatment" is morally wrong. It degrades the value of citizenship if foreign investors have equal rights, or even greater rights than citizens, as they do under NAFTA. In most parts of the world people are not allowed to move from country to country looking for the best job unless they first get a visa. But "national treatment" is the passport which allows corporations unrestricted access. That is what globalization is all about – to give corporations greater rights than people.

In Canada's case, national treatment is the operative clause in our last will and testament. It allows American corporations to invest in Canada without conditions and without limits. We can no longer say, "you are welcome if you invest in Thunder Bay, Trois-Rivières or Powell River." We can no longer say, "you are welcome if you export a certain percentage of your output, or do some research and development in Canada or promise to leave the technology behind if you pull up stakes and move out." No conditions can be applied!

Similarly, we cannot impose limits. We can't say, "you can't buy more than 50% of our forest industries" because the treaty says they can buy them all. And we can't say, "you can't own more than 60% of our oil and gas reserves" because the treaty allows them to buy and own them all – the direction in which we are headed.

HAS "FREE TRADE" BEEN GOOD FOR CANADA?

Supporters of the FTA usually cite increased trade between Canada and the U.S. as proof positive that the FTA has been a big contributor to Canada's prosperity. Exports to the U.S., including Puerto Rico and the Virgin Islands, increased from $108 billion in 1989 to $360 billion in 2001.[6] Also total exports of goods and services increased from 25.6% of GDP in 1989 to 45.6% in 2000.[7] So, they say, much of our "prosperity" for the last decade can be attributed to the FTA.

Others say that those figures lie; or, at the very least, they don't tell the whole truth. A new study by Industry Canada concludes that the weak dollar has done more to boost exports to the U.S. over the past decade than the free trade agreements. The FTA and NAFTA did boost exports, but, "the impact of (free trade) .... was modest," as the two trade deals accounted for only 9% of the increase in exports to the U.S.[8] Furthermore the data on Canada's exports to the United States includes shipments to Third World countries via the United States, which means that exports to the U.S. are somewhat overstated while trade with other countries is understated.[9]

Chart No.1
Automotive Trade with U.S.

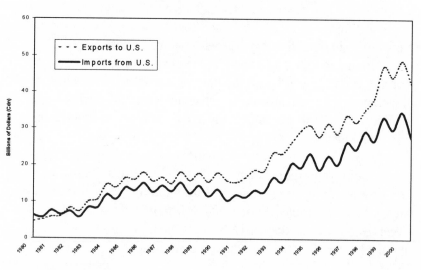

Source: Statistics Canada

Canada's biggest gains in exports to the U.S. since the FTA was signed have been in automobiles and energy. In both cases the connection to the FTA, if any, has been minimal. In the case of automobiles, the increase is largely attributable to the Auto Pact which represented Canadian "protectionism" at its best and most successful. This advantage was amplified, of course, by the dramatic fall in the relative value of the Canadian dollar. Chart No. 1 tells the story.

These figures are bloated by more than $12 billion due to double accounting. Car parts are counted as imports or exports as they cross the border to be installed in a car, and counted a second time when the completed car is subsequently shipped back across the same border.

The most dramatic increase in Canadian exports to the U.S. has been electricity, natural gas and crude oil. This is due to the almost insatiable demand for energy south of the border and exports will continue to rise with or without NAFTA. Chart 2 shows the trend which reflects higher prices as well as increased volume.

Chart No.2
Energy Exports to U.S.

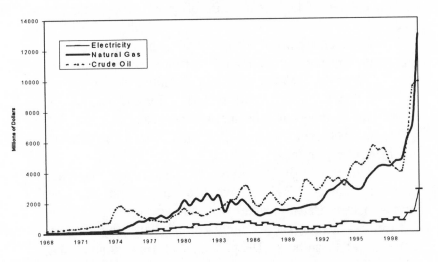

Source: Statistics Canada

As for the increase in exports as a percentage of total GDP, which "free traders" tout in support of their solution, this is attributable, to a significant extent, to the fact that both federal and provincial governments strangled the domestic economy in the 1990s. They cut back just about every activity that could be cut back, and this took its toll. So although the gross trade figures look encouraging, they are primarily camouflage. The real story is that we are no better off than we would have been without the FTA and NAFTA. And if you look at the whole picture you may conclude that we are worse off – much worse!

FALLING BEHIND

Our living standards have fallen consistently behind the Americans since 1989, when the free trade agreement came into effect. Ottawa's Centre for the Study of Living Standards calculates that Canada's per capita GDP fell to 79% of the U.S. level in 2000, from 86% in 1989.[10] As William Thorsell, former Editor-in-Chief of the *Globe and Mail*, and one of the strongest supporters of the FTA, admitted in his column "Second thoughts on free trade", "We have failed to keep pace with the Americans on job growth and productivity over the period as a whole, which starkly contradicts the predictions of those of us who fought for free trade."[11]

True enough. Although total exports and imports increased, the number of manufacturing establishments and jobs fell sharply. Wages were flat or falling down even in the so-called winning export sectors. By the end of the decade the number of jobs in manufacturing was still 6% below its 1989 level. Chart 3 plots total exports and imports, and manufacturing jobs.

Evidence that the trade expansion and economic integration under NAFTA have had an adverse effect on employment in Canada comes from the government itself, in the form of a little-known study commissioned by Industry Canada. The authors, Dungan and Murphy, found that, while business sector exports grew quickly, import growth also kept pace. At the same time, the import content per unit of exports also grew markedly, while the domestic content per unit of exports fell. This means that employment (direct and indirect) in export industries rose from 19.6% of total business sector employment in 1989, to 28.3% in 1997. The rapid rise in imports, however, displaced (or destroyed) even more employment. The job-displacing effect of imports rose steadily from an equivalent of 21.1% of total business employment in 1989, to 32.7% in 1997. The authors conclude: "Imports are displacing 'relatively' more jobs than exports are adding."[12]

Chart No. 3
Canada-U.S. Exports and Imports and
Manufacturing Employment

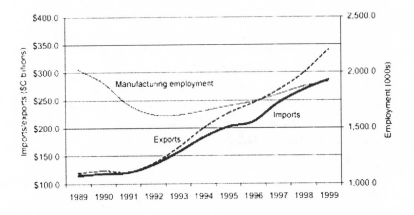

Source: Statistics Canada

What did this mean in terms of actual jobs created and destroyed? Bruce Campbell of the Canadian Centre for Policy Alternatives derived these numbers from Dungan and Murphy's data. The result is striking. Between 1989 and 1997, about 870,700 export jobs were created, but during the same period 1,147,100 jobs were destroyed by imports. Thus, Canada's trade boom resulted in a net destruction of 276,000 jobs.[13]

- Our family farms are being squeezed out of business by the market power of giant U.S. agribusinesses. While Canada's agriculture exports grew by $6 billion between 1993 and 1999, net farm income declined by $600 million over the same period instead of rising by $1.4 billion as Agri-Food Canada had predicted. Since NAFTA, the rate of Canadian farm bankruptcies and delinquent loans is five times that before NAFTA.

- As already pointed out, ownership and control of thousands of Canadian companies is being lost.

- Family incomes have been squeezed since the FTA was signed and although I would be the last to attribute this entirely to the FTA it does prove that the agreement was not the panacea its promoters claimed it would be.

In summation, the average Canadian is not better off as a result of "Free Trade" and our standard of living has fallen further and further behind the U.S. since we surrendered so much of our sovereignty. That is worrisome enough. But it pales in significance to the fact that we are losing our country. And if we don't do an about-turn, it will soon be lost forever!

TWO YEARS TO THE POINT OF NO RETURN

In about two years Canada will reach the point of no return after which annexation by the United States will become inevitable. It might be three years but it is unlikely to be more than four at the outside. There are several reasons for this assessment. The first, and most obvious, is the rate of sale of Canada's core companies. If the government continues to relax the rules on foreign ownership it won't be too long before there will be nothing of significance left to sell. Canada will be little more than an empty shell.

When ownership moves outside Canada so do the best, decision-making, high-value jobs. Many of our best and brightest move to follow the most exciting and most rewarding opportunities. Also the tax base is being seriously eroded. Foreign-owned companies find ways of paying minimum tax in the host country. Consequently loss of ownership means less revenue for public services, which affects our standard of living.

Second, and directly related, is the continuing presence of the "national treatment" clause. The FTA and NAFTA can be abrogated (cancelled) with six months' notice. But the globalizers, including the Canadian government, have been trying to entrench "national treatment" for a longer period. They attempted to pass a Multilateral Agreement on Investment (MAI) binding the 29 countries of the Organization for Economic Cooperation and Development (OECD) to this clause for five years, plus fifteen years grandfather rights, for a total of 20 years. If the MAI had been signed it would have been "game over" for Canada and there would have been no point in writing this book.

Several dissident groups, with an unprecedented internet campaign, won that battle but the war rages on. The European Union is trying to entrench national treatment under the World Trade Organization, while Canada and the U.S. are pushing it under the Free Trade Area of the Americas (FTAA). The original timetable for completion of negotiations was 2005, but the new U.S. administration is reported to be hoping for an earlier completion. When the treaty is signed, in 2004 or 2005, Canada will be a dead duck – or perhaps a "dead loonie" would be more appropriate.

To people who think I am an alarmist, I can only say that I fervently wish that was the case. But my record for projecting trend lines is impeccable. Three examples from earlier days in politics will illustrate.

As a neophyte MP I was invited to attend the ceremony the day the first pile was driven for Toronto's Yonge Street subway. After the event we were invited to cruise Toronto harbour on the ferryboat Sam McBride. Somehow I wound up in the wheelhouse with the chairman of the Toronto Transportation Commission (TTC), William McBrien,[14] where I spent about half-an-hour trying to persuade him to extend the subway north from Eglinton, which was its final destination. But he was adamant. No!

The TTC wasn't sure the line was going to be successful. Rebuffed on the extension, I then urged him to buy the right-of-way so it would be available for future expansion. Again the answer was a firm "no". Eventually the TTC – read "taxpayers" – wound up paying as much as $250,000 an acre for land which was available for $400 at the time.

Speaking on the 1955 budget in the House of Commons I talked about the inadequacy of evacuation routes which would allow Torontonians to exit the city in the event of a national emergency. In a specific reference to highway 401, which was still known at the time as the Toronto by-pass, I pointed out that the four-lane project would be inadequate 48 hours after it was opened.[15] Was there ever any doubt?

Then in the mid-1960s, I made a speech – I think it was to the Toronto Junior Board of Trade – in which I predicted that housing prices in Toronto, which were then less than $20,000, on average, would be about $225,000, on average, in 25 years. Now, more than 35 years later, I still meet people who heard that speech and who tell me frankly, "Hellyer, when I walked out of that room I said the man is cuckoo, totally bananas, and should be confined to a place for the mentally challenged," as they call it now. Actually, I was just a tiny bit – dare I use the word – conservative in my projection, with average prices reaching $225,000 in slightly under 25 years.[16]

One does not need either the gift of prophecy or a crystal ball to make reliable predictions. All you have to do is look carefully at a trend line, and then sit down and estimate where it is likely to be a few years hence. Perhaps it is best described as educated guesswork.

Today, I regret to say, the trend line for Canada is ultimate annexation by the United States. I don't know when that will occur but I do know that we are getting close to the point of no return. Soon, annexation will be inevitable, and there will be nothing anyone including a future, more enlightened government, can do to stop it.

FOR WHOM THE BELLS TOLL

If I were the only one to be concerned I would have to take a long hard look in the mirror. But I am not alone. In a telephone conversation with Willard Z. (Bud) Estey, former Justice of the Supreme Court of Canada, in the summer of 1999, he said: "Paul, the country is going down the drain by the hour, as we speak."[17]

In an article entitled "Canada is sliding to ruin: Royal Bank", the then chief economist and now member of parliament for Markham, John McCallum, said he was disturbed during a recent meeting of eminent Canadians, including Order of Canada recipients, when it was suggested Canada might not exist in a generation or two.[18]

Just hours before he resigned as Chairman of Xerox Canada Ltd., Kevin Francis, its CEO for more than 28 years, said Canada is in danger of becoming a satellite of U.S. multinationals. "Increasingly, if you look at the Canadian economy today, if you're not working in the high-tech arena for an American multinational, then you're slinging burgers at an American franchise. At the high end and the low end of the Canadian economy, most of our economic growth is being controlled outside the country."[19]

The venerable Canadian nationalist Peter Newman has sounded repeated warnings. His most recent, which appeared in the January 8, 2001, issue of *Maclean's* magazine, was titled "The End of Canada? Measures to expand free trade will inevitably lead to the end of first our dollar – and then our sovereignty."[20] After reading the article my only question was why *Maclean's* included the "?" in the title.

Of all the articles on the subject, probably the most pessimistic was one by Steven Pearlstein which appeared in the *Washington Post* on September 5, 2000, under the title "O Canada! A National Swan Song?"[21] Pearlstein, who had just finished a tour as the *Post's* Canadian correspondent, had attended a meeting of 200 of Canada's most influential citizens at Toronto's Royal York Hotel to consider the country's prospects in the global economy. Pearlstein's assessment: "As the chieftains, university presidents and government officials rose to speak [amid the ornate frescoes and gilded mouldings meant to give expression to Canada's 19th century ambitions], it soon became clear that many were haunted by a more disturbing question. Would there even be a Canada in 25 years, or would the country become, for all practical purposes, the 51st American state?"

The article was paraphrased in the *National Post* the following day[22] and subsequently ridiculed in an editorial entitled "The 51st state? Never", where it said, "... a full melding of the two nations is political science fiction."[23] I thought as I read the editorial that only the *Post*, whose forte is fiction, could possibly come to that conclusion. Apart from the *Post* there was no comment that I saw. The silence was so deafening that it was as if Canadian opinion makers had been drugged. There were no ringing cries of "wake up, or give up."

The complacency appears to extend to the population at large. A survey by EKOS Research Associates, published in the *National Post*, June 4, 2001, showed that nearly one Canadian in two expects Canada to be part of a North American union within 10 years while one in four believe the country will be absorbed by the United States within 20 years.[24]

I would like to make it very clear at this point that I am not anti-American. I respect and admire the American people. But I have a profound distrust of the American government and its foreign policy which is dictated by American corporate interests rather than the interests of the American people. There are many Americans, including David Korten, Noam Chomsky and Ralph Nader, who are similarly distrustful of their government's motives and the rise of corporatism. The sad fact, which many observers have long suspected, is that we are all being manipulated by a very small but elite group which one could argue is even more powerful than the U.S. government, and which is using that government as its agent in establishing the New World Order.

CHAPTER 2

THE NEW WORLD (DIS)ORDER

"We are grateful to the Washington Post, the New York Times, Time Magazine and other great publications whose directors have attended our meetings and respected their promise of discretion for almost forty years. It would have been impossible for us to develop our plan for the world if we had been subjected to the lights of publicity during those years. But the world is now more sophisticated and prepared to march towards a world government. The supranational sovereignty of an intellectual elite and world bankers is surely preferable to the national auto-determination practised in past centuries."

David Rockefeller[1]

There you have it! In one paragraph David Rockefeller sums up what the New World Order is all about – the substitution of elite rule for democracy. Rockefeller denies the accuracy of the above statement, secure in the knowledge that there are no verbatim records of the highly secretive Bilderberger meetings, but I believe it is authentic because virtually every move he has made in the last 40 years lends credence to its authenticity.

It is impossible to understand globalization and the New World Order unless you know who is behind it – whose agenda it is. A little digging indicates that there are a number of organizations involved, of which three are paramount. They are the Council on Foreign Relations, centred in New York City, the Bilderbergers, the most exclusive and secretive of the three, and the Trilateral Commission, which is the most open to public scrutiny. Not surprisingly, there is an interconnection between both the players and the objectives of the three groups, although they are not identical.

THE COUNCIL ON FOREIGN RELATIONS

The Council on Foreign Relations (CFR or Council) is the oldest of the three. Although it was active in the 1920s and 1930s, it only came into a position of great influence with the outbreak of World War II. As early as October, 1940, its Economic and Financial Group drafted a memorandum outlining a comprehensive policy, "... to set forth the political, military, territorial and economic requirements of the United States in its potential leadership of the non-German world area including the United Kingdom itself as well as the Western hemisphere and Far East."[2]

The "Grand Area", as the non-German bloc was called in 1941, was insufficiently grand. The preferred ideal was all-inclusive – one world economy dominated by the United States.[3] It was at this stage that there was a virtual merger of the Council and the U.S. State Department which, in late 1941, created a special committee to consider positive planning. The Advisory Committee on Positive Foreign Policy, on which Council members played important roles, set the stage for key decisions that would affect the post-war world.

The Council influenced plans for international economic institutions including the International Monetary Fund (IMF) and the International Bank for Reconstruction and Development (World Bank). It was also deeply involved in the creation of the United Nations. At a meeting in May, 1942, one of the Council members, Isaiah Bowman, argued that the United States had to exercise the strength to assure "security", and at the same time "avoid conventional forms of imperialism."[4] The way to do this, he suggested, was to make the exercise of that power international in character through a United Nations body.[5]

It was clear at all times that the purpose of the Grand Area and later world hegemony was to support an expanding U.S. economy – to provide it with raw materials and markets for its products. This was labelled the "national interest." It was equally clear that the "national interest" was the interest of the ruling elite whose members comprised the Council. The real interests of the majority of rank-and-file Americans was never a factor in the equation.

THE BILDERBERGERS

Bilderberg was the brainchild of Dr. Joseph Retinger, a top aide to General Wladyslaw Sikorski, head of the Polish government in exile in London. Even during World War II he suggested regular meetings of the foreign ministers of Continental countries and established close relationships with men who were to become post-war leaders.

After the war, Retinger explained his concern for European unification in a meeting at Chatham House, home of the Royal Society on International Affairs, the British equivalent of the Council on Foreign Relations. His recipe for a divided Europe, which had rejected both Hitler's New World and communism, was to move towards a federal union of neighbouring European countries, in which the states would "relinquish part of their sovereignty."[6]

The idea was not new, of course, but Retinger gave it currency at a critical time in the post-war development of Europe. He was also a catalyst in establishing closer ties between Europe and America at a time when there was a lot of anti-Americanism on the continent. It was as a result of this process that the group which became known as the Bilderbergers evolved.

The name comes from the group's first meeting place, the Hotel de Bilderberg of Oosterbeek, Holland, in May 1954. The meeting was chaired by Prince Bernhard of Holland who, along with Paul Rykens of Unilever, drew up the original list of participants, two from each country, with representatives of business, banking, politics, academia, etc. with a fair balance of conservative and liberal views that were not too far left – as perceived by the Prince and the steering committee chosen by him. The group was pragmatic enough to ensure that their views would carry weight regardless of who formed the government of the day.

One should not discount the positive influence the group has had on inter-governmental relations and the resolution of international problems. It has contributed to just about every major debate the West has faced. Membership, which is not officially acknowledged, reads like a Who's Who of power and influence. President John F. Kennedy virtually staffed the State Department with Bilderberg alumni, including Secretary of State Dean Rusk and Under-Secretary of State George W. Ball.

In fact it is only the elite members of society who are asked to attend. They are people who, as a result of their position, power or influence, can help propagate the Bilderberg consensus on any subject. While this has sometimes been a good thing, it can also be a bad thing because Bilderbergers tend to equate their personal interests with the public interest. The New World Order, with its seamless market and vanishing borders, would, for most of them, enhance their power and wealth. They are probably incapable of believing that it would be bad for the world's masses.

THE TRILATERAL COMMISSION

The youngest of the three major groups pushing globalization is the Trilateral Commission, which was officially founded in July, 1973. Its roots can be traced to Zbigniew Brzezinski, then a Columbia University professor. He wrote a series of papers acknowledging Japan's increasing power and influence on the world stage and then organized the Tripartite Studies under the auspices of the Brookings Institution, known in Washington as the think-tank for Democratic administrations.

These studies helped convince David Rockefeller that trilateralism could be a useful instrument in building a community of interest between North America, Western Europe and Japan at a time when relations between the three were deteriorating. When he and Brzezinski presented the idea of a trilateral arrangement to the Bilderberg annual meeting in 1972 it received an enthusiastic response – the endorsement Rockefeller needed to follow up and make the dream a reality.

This organization is the most open about its aims and objectives. It is elitist and anti-democratic. A 1975 report entitled "The Crisis of Democracy: Report on the Governability of Democracies to the Trilateral Commission," states: "The vulnerability of democratic government in the United States comes not primarily from external threats, though such threats are real, not from internal subversion from the left or right, although both possibilities could exist, but rather from internal dynamics of democracy itself in a highly educated, mobilized, and participant society."[7] Wow, the principal danger to democratic governments is democracy. That is a concept that you have to dig deep to come up with. What about the danger to democracy of actions taken by governments "elected" by the people, but only after being chosen and "installed" in positions of leadership by elite groups like the Trilateral Commission?

The political power of the Trilats, a convenient abbreviation I will use for the Commission, and its sister organizations the Council on Foreign Relations and the Bilderbergers, is ominous. When they became concerned about the protectionist measures of the Nixon administration, they began to look around for someone to replace him. The name of Jimmy Carter appeared on a short list of three and he was the one who ultimately got the nod. It was the Trilat connections in the media who helped the obscure peanut farmer, and member of the Trilateral Commission, achieve national prominence and become a leading contender for the Democratic Party nomination for president. The operation succeeded as planned and when Carter became president he named seventeen Trilats to important positions in his administration.[8]

When, after four years, the Trilats became somewhat disillusioned with Carter, they decided to replace him with another one of their own, George Bush.[9] A small problem arose when Bush ran for the Replication nomination. Opponents in five states ran full page ads saying, "The same people who gave you Jimmy Carter are giving you George Bush." In the face of this setback the Trilats had to settle for a Reagan-Bush ticket and George Bush had to bide his time while Reagan, who had been looked upon with some skepticism, really came through for them with the Canada-U.S. Free Trade Agreement.

Later, after George Bush finally had his turn, and his era drew to a close, the Trilats picked another one of their own, Bill Clinton, to be the Democratic standard bearer. Clinton's colourful personal life made the road to stardom a somewhat rocky one but, with the help of his powerful allies, he prevailed.

Clinton's pay-off to his benefactors was profound and continuing. Most dramatic was his successful negotiation of NAFTA in order to provide the U.S. Round Table on Business (and Canadian business, too) unrestricted access to an unlimited supply of cheap Mexican labour. This process has been ably recorded in *The Selling of "Free Trade": NAFTA, Washington and the Subversion of U.S. Democracy*, by John R. MacArthur, publisher of *Harper's Magazine*.[10] It is a case history of the manipulation of Congress which anyone interested in politics should read.

Of even greater long-term significance, Clinton transformed the Democratic Party from one that sometimes listened to and cared about the concerns of traditional allies including trade unionists, environmentalists, the poor and social activists, into just another party only marginally but not too significantly different from the Republican Party. His robust promotion of "Free Trade", including the proposed Free Trade Area of the Americas, has robbed U.S. nationalists, and other thoughtful Americans concerned about the serious loss of sovereignty, from any effective voice in determining their future. The Clinton rightward shift was an answer to the Trilats' prayers.

Only the election of someone like George W. Bush could make Clinton look, in retrospect, like a moderate. G.W. Bush follows closely in his father's footsteps and quickens the pace to the right. His solid support for the National Missile Defence (son of Star Wars) sounds like sabre-rattling to the peacemakers but is music to the ears of U.S. militarists and industrialists. And anyone who doesn't think that the limited defence against "rogue states" won't evolve into a full-fledged anti-missile shield, triggering a world-wide arms race, should be sent to a school for the naïve.

The new president has infuriated environmentalists and thoughtful people world-wide by declaring that the U.S. will not adhere to the Kyoto Protocol. In the classic struggle between the present and the future, the present won. Today's profits are given a higher priority than the protection of the planet.

If this were not enough to demonstrate the over-whelming power of the oil industry – which just happens to own vast coal deposits – the president has invented another "energy crisis." This one is just as artificial as the last one, but it provides the backdrop for an exploration invasion of the Arctic National Wildlife Refuge in Alaska. Also, the demand for a continental energy policy is designed to guarantee that Canadian and Mexican surpluses are available to offset American deficits.

George W. Bush has already proven that he will push the Trilat agenda with all the power and muscle available to him even though that agenda includes the demise of the kind of democracy envisioned by the Fathers of the American Constitution. Treaties negotiated on behalf of transnational corporations will crimp the power of Congress. Unelected, unaccountable panels set up under NAFTA and the World Trade Organization (WTO) will make decisions in secret which cannot be overturned by the Supreme Court of the United States. In other words government of, by and for the people is on its death bed and it won't be long before the coroner makes it official.

THE PROPAGANDA MACHINE

It is impossible to separate the organizations behind the Global Agenda from the ideology, or perhaps theology would be more accurate, on which its doctrine is based. It is variously referred to as "*laissez-faire*", "neo-conservatism", "neo-liberalism" and "la pensée unique" (the dominant or single mind-set). It could also be called Darwinian economics because only the most gifted and powerful members of the species can survive its mechanical process of selection and exclusion.

Call it what you like, this now-dominant doctrine did not originate in heaven. It has been carefully cultivated over several decades by a closely-knit band of individuals who recognized the power of ideas and decided to use that power for their own advantage. The well-known researcher, writer and thinker, Susan George, sums up their methodology as follows:

"The neo-liberals thus conceived their successful strategy, recruiting and rewarding thinkers and writers, raising funds to found and to sustain a broad range of institutions at the forefront of the 'conservative revolution'. This revolution began in the United States but, like the rest of American culture, has spread worldwide and influences politics throughout Europe and elsewhere. The doctrines of the International Monetary Fund, The World Bank and the World Trade Organization are indistinguishable from those of the neo-liberal credo."[11]

Here are some capsule profiles of the most influential institutions and think-tanks.

"The American Enterprise Institute was founded in 1943 by a group of anti-New Deal businessmen. It pioneered intellectual public relations in the 1950s and 1960s, working directly with members of Congress, the Federal bureaucracy and the media.

"The Heritage Foundation is the best known think-tank because of its close association with Ronald Reagan. A week after his electoral victory, Heritage's director handed Reagan's staff a thousand page document of policy advice, called Mandate for Leadership, fruit of the labors of 250 neo-liberal experts. Their recommendations were duly distributed throughout the new administration; most became law. The Foundation's Annual Guide lists 1500 neo-liberal public policy experts in 70 different areas – the harried journalist need only telephone to get a quote.

"Heritage's success has inspired the creation of 37 mini-Heritages across the U.S., creating synergy, an illusion of diversity and the impression that experts quoted actually represent a broad spectrum of views.

"Some other, smaller, think-tanks include the venerable Hoover Institution on War, Revolution and Peace, founded at Stanford University in California, in 1919, to study communism. The Cato Institute in Washington, is libertarian, advocating minimalist government and specializing in studies on privatization. The Manhattan Institute for Policy Research, founded in 1978 by William Casey, later director of the CIA, specializes in the critique of government income-redistribution programmes.

"Outside the U.S.A., the neo-liberal network is less formal but no less effective in ideological guerrilla tactics (in the U.K. they called themselves 'Mrs. Thatcher's commandos'). London houses the Centre for Policy Studies; the anti-Statist Institute of Economic Affairs, and the Adam Smith Institute (ASI) which has probably done more to promote privatization than any other institution anywhere. The ASI brags that over 200 measures developed by its 'Omega Project' were put into practice by Mrs. Thatcher. Its experts have also advised the World Bank extensively on privatization programmes in the Bank's client countries."[12]

Even Canada is not immune. We have the Fraser Institute in British Columbia and the C.D. Howe Institute with its headquarters in Toronto. Reports from these organizations are treated as independent research by media outlets which have become increasingly conservative over the past decade or so as their views have been moulded by the deluge of neo-liberal press releases, books and lectures.

Recently, a number of small think-tanks have sprouted like mushrooms under names like the Montreal Economic Institute. It conveniently attempted to discredit the ideas held by people opposed to globalization just prior to the Summit of the Americas, while proclaiming to be an independent economic research institute. When asked to provide a list of its financial donors, so the integrity of its claim to independence could be verified, it declined to do so.[13]

As Susan George points out there seems to be no shortage of funds for think-tanks and other institutions with the "right" point of view. "In the early days, the William Volker Fund saved the shaky magazines, financed the books published at Chicago, paid the bills for the influential Foundation for Economic Education and funded meetings in U.S. universities. It also paid the expenses for Americans travelling to Switzerland to the first meeting of the Mount Pelerin Society, founded in 1947 by economist Friedrich von Hayek.

"As the right wing movement grew additional funds were required. So it was a big coup when the American Enterprise Institute was granted $300,000 by the Ford Foundation in 1972, a large sum at that time. Numerous family foundations have poured money into the production and dissemination of their ideas. The Bradley Foundation spends nearly all of its annual income ($28 million in 1994) promoting neo-liberal causes. Foundations like Coors (brewery), Scaife or Mellon (steel), and especially Olin (chemicals, munitions) finance chairs in some of America's most prestigious universities. Their occupants are carefully chosen, in the words of critic Jon Weiner, 'to strengthen the economic, political and cultural institutions upon which ... private enterprise is based.' Olin has spent over $55 million on these efforts and the list of its grantees reads like a Who's Who of the academic right.

"An anecdote recounted by Weiner illustrates how the ideological self-promotion system works. In 1988, Allan Bloom, Director of the University of Chicago's Olin Centre for Inquiry into the Theory and Practice of Democracy ($3.6 million grant from Olin) invites a State Department official to give a paper. The speaker proclaims total victory for the West and for neo-liberal values in the Cold War. His paper is immediately published in *The National Interest* ($1 million Olin subsidy) edited by Irving Kristol ($376,000 grant as Olin Distinguished Professor at New York University Graduate School of Business).

"Kristol simultaneously publishes 'responses' to the paper: one by himself, one by Bloom (as above); and one by Samuel Huntington ($1.4 million for the Olin Institute for Strategic Studies at Harvard). This completely artificial, engineered 'debate' is picked up by the *New York Times*, the *Washington Post* and *Time* magazine. Today almost everyone has heard of Francis Fukuyama and *The End of History* a best-seller in several languages."[14]

The Canadian media bombard us with neo-liberal ideas daily. Of the many outlets none is quite so blatant as the *National Post*, a progeny of Conrad Black, a long-time Bilderberger. So it is not surprising that the *Post* is nothing if not a propaganda sheet for the Bilderberg, New World Order, point of view. Periodic headlines in the *Post* trumpet Canada's miserable performance, relative to our American cousins, planting the seed that perhaps we should either emulate them or just pack it in and add our fading star to the Stars and Stripes.

Like most tracts selling "religion", it is done with the fervour of the "True Believer". Editorials by Terence Corcoran, Editor-in Chief of the *Financial Post* section of the paper, and by Peter Foster, are entirely predictable. The same applies to their regular columnists like William Watson, Andrew Coyne and others. Infrequent pieces by Linda McQuaig and Murray Dobbin are welcome relief, but their effect is comparable to pouring a pitcher full of crystal clear water into the muddy Toronto Harbour after a big storm.

The bottom line is that the neo-liberal globalizers have put together a propaganda machine unprecedented in the history of the world. That is how they have convinced people all over the world that globalization is inevitable and, by inference, good, without any solid data or scientific evidence to back up their pretentious and self-serving claims. They propose a system that has been tried before and proven to be both unstable and unsustainable. Still it is being rammed down our collective consciousness one more time. The only hope is better ideas propagated by whatever means are available to people who are neither rich nor powerful.

P.S. Literally hours before this book went to press, Conrad Black sold his remaining 50 percent interest in the *National Post* to Israel "Izzy" Asper's CanWest Global Communications conglomerate. It will be interesting to see how much the staunchly pro-Liberal Asper family will change the editorial policy of the *Post*.

CHAPTER 3

A MEANS TO AN END

"The public and leaders of most countries continue to live in a mental universe which no longer exists – a world of separate nations – and have great difficulty thinking in terms of global perspectives and interdependence – toward a renovated international system ."

Trilateral Task Force Report, 1977

It is all well and good for the Trilats to decree that the nation state is obsolete, and that the New World Order is one that will be governed by economics alone, but they have no direct power to effect the change. Their power lies with their influence on governments, the means of mass communication, philanthropic foundations, international financial institutions and other organizations. These are the institutions which, collectively, have enough clout to unwind the sinews of democracy and substitute plutocracy – a re-incarnated feudalism of the elite.

The Trilats use political leaders to achieve their objectives. They persuade them to push trade agreements, for example, and sell them on the basis that free trade will increase the living standards of the masses. That is the kind of popular appeal that political leaders are looking for. Who cares if the fine print includes some uncertainties concerning sovereignty? Not one person in ten thousand, including politicians, will read the text of the agreement and consequently they will be unaware of any sinister implications that may be lurking there.

Although the Israel-U.S. Free Trade Agreement was first, it was the Canada-U.S. Free Trade Agreement which has had such a profound affect on Canada, and later the world. Although "national treatment" had made its debut in the World Trade Organization when it was still the General Agreement on Tariffs and Trade (GATT), it was the bilateral trade agreements which first introduced it to the realm of investment. Justified in the name of a "level playing field" it is, in fact, a major erosion of national sovereignty. All of a sudden you see international corporations replace governments in the driver's seat.

It is not surprising, then, that in the run-up to the 1988 election the Business Council on National Issues (BCNI), dominated by transnational corporations, would spend millions on advertising in support of free trade. The power of the purse was unleashed on behalf of one side of the argument. When confronted with the apparent unfairness the stock reply is, "everyone is equally free to support their views by buying advertisements." That is technically true but, realistically, it is humbug. One side has all the money so there is no level playing field when it comes to moulding public opinion.

NAFTA WAS WORSE

A book entitled *Building a Partnership*,[1] is a collection of statements and recollections by the Canadian and U.S. "Trade Warriors" who negotiated the FTA. When they met to celebrate the tenth anniversary of the agreement, they patted themselves on the back for pioneering a succession of subsequent treaties beginning with NAFTA.

The FTA certainly helped pave the way for NAFTA, but the real driving force behind the treaty was the U.S. Round Table on Business. Its members wanted access to an unlimited supply of cheap Mexican labour. President Bill Clinton was already in the Trilats' debt for choosing him as a preferred candidate for the presidency, and helping to get him elected despite formidable odds; but he was then looking ahead to the next election and his obvious need to look to big business for gobs of money for his campaign.

So he played their game with all of the skill of the super salesman he really was. He had to win over, or at least neutralize, a Democratic Party which had traditionally held other values. His series of moves would have done credit to a grand master at chess. But there would be a considerable long-range cost to the American people.

NAFTA's CHAPTER 11

Not only did NAFTA achieve its twin aims of unrestricted access to cheap labour and of putting downward pressure on Canadian and U.S. wages, it introduced another profoundly important provision to limit the power of governments. Chapter 11, which Canadians often confuse with the U.S. bankruptcy protection law, is a new disputes settlement provision for the exclusive benefit of corporations at the expense of national governments.

We are told that this provision was included by Canadian and U.S. negotiators for the protection of their transnationals reluctant to invest in Mexico for fear of having their investment affected by some arbitrary action on the part of the Mexican government. If that was their objective, they were successful. But either they were naïve, and didn't recognize a two-way street when they saw one, or they were duplicitous and more concerned about corporations than citizens because the most important consequences have been those affecting the Canadian and U.S. governments – especially Canadian.

The net effect of Chapter 11 is that when any level of government, federal, provincial or municipal, passes or amends a law or regulation which affects a foreign investor's profits, future profits, or potential profits, they can sue the host government for damages. Foreign investors have greater rights in the host country than citizens of that country, which is absurd. It is not surprising that they take full advantage of their preferred status. Canada, the U.S. and Mexico have all been sued by foreign corporations.

THE ETHYL CASE

The Ethyl case was the first against Canada and it is worth mentioning here because it provides a dramatic illustration of our loss of sovereignty. The Canadian parliament passed a law banning the importation into Canada and the distribution within Canada of the gasoline additive methylcyclopentadienyl manganese tricarbonyl (MMT). The Ethyl Corporation of the U.S. sued the Canadian government for US$251 million on the grounds of lost profits and damaged reputation. The case would be heard by a three-person panel whose decision would be final.

When its lawyers advised that it would likely lose the case, the Canadian government settled. It paid US$13 million, about CD$19 million, in compensation for legal fees and other costs. Far worse, as part of the settlement agreement, two cabinet ministers were required to read statements to the effect that MMT is not harmful either to the environment or to health, and this despite evidence that low-level exposure to airborne manganese is linked to nervous-system problems and attention-deficit disorder among children.

The most far-reaching consequence, however, is that the Canadian parliament was required to repeal the law. What kind of democracy is it where a foreign corporation can dictate to the parliament of Canada which laws it can pass, and those it cannot pass, without horrendous financial consequences?

Canada lost another case to S.D. Myers Inc. of Tallmadge, Ohio, which launched a suit claiming compensation for a 15-month ban on the export of polychlorinated biphenyls (PCBs) dating back to 1995.

Other suits are pending. Sun Belt Water Inc. of California is suing us for between US$1.5 and US$10.5 billion, because we won't let it sell our water. And United Parcel Services (UPS) is asking for US$225 million because it claims Canada Post is cross-subsidizing its Purolator courier service.

CASES AGAINST THE U.S.

Until November, 1999, all of the actions under NAFTA were launched by U.S. corporations. Then the Canadian funeral giant Loewen Group Inc., of Burnaby, British Columbia, billed the U.S. government for losses sustained in a Mississippi court which ordered it to pay US$500 million in damages in a contract dispute with the O'Keefe family, operators of a small funeral and insurance business in the state.

The O'Keefe suit was subsequently settled for $150 million but the case left Loewen financially crippled. So it sued the U.S. on the grounds that Mississippi violated acceptable standards of justice by forcing it to post a bond equal to 125% of the damage award.

Reaction was swift, and predictable. "This case is an all-out attack on democracy," Joan Claybrook, president of Public Citizen, a Washington-based consumer advocacy group founded by Ralph Nader, charged. "It would open a huge, back-door way for corporations to get protection from their liabilities in a way they have been unable to win in two decades of lobbying in Congress."[2]

The claim for damages constitutes an attempted "end run" around U.S. jury verdicts, Ms. Claybrook said. "We cannot stand by and allow NAFTA to be used as a broom for a sore loser to sweep justice aside."[3]

Without commenting on the merits of the case which appeared, at a distance, to be anything but just, one must agree with Ms. Claybrook's concern. The issue, in reality, is sovereignty. The provisions of NAFTA constitute a serious intrusion on national sovereignty and regardless of the outcome of these cases they will be just the first of hundreds if the same "right" is entrenched in other multilateral treaties.

In another more recent case Methanex, a Canadian company, is suing the U.S. government because the state of California legislated that MTBE, a gasoline additive, be banned by 2002. This substance has been associated with neurotoxicology effects, and is highly soluble in water. Methanex is using NAFTA to sue the state of California for US$970 million for "expropriated" future profits.

MEXICO IS NOT EXEMPT

The case which caused greatest alarm amongst defenders of states' or provincial rights has been Metalclad vs. Mexico. In January, 1997, this U.S.-based waste disposal company filed a complaint with the International Center for the Settlement of Investment Disputes (ICSID), alleging that the Mexican state of San Luis Potosi violated a number of provisions of NAFTA when it prevented the company from opening its waste disposal plant. Metalclad took over the facility, which had a history of contaminating local ground water, with the obligation that it clean up pre-existing contaminants.

After an environmental impact assessment revealed that the site was over an ecologically sensitive underground alluvial stream, the governor refused to allow Metalclad to re-open the facility. Eventually the site was declared part of a 600,000 acre ecological zone. Metalclad claimed that this action effectively expropriated its future expected profits and asked for $90 million in damages – a sum larger than the combined annual income of every family in the county where the facility was located.[4]

A NAFTA tribunal awarded Metalclad US$16.7 million after ruling that the treaty applies equally to sub-national governments and that matters such as environmental impact, the performance record of the plaintiff and public opposition to the project were not relevant to the decision of the local government.

In a precedent setting move the Mexican government appealed the decision which was presumably binding and not subject to review by the courts. Nevertheless the case was heard in Vancouver, B.C., by a Canadian judge. He reduced the award from US$16.7 million to about US$15.9 million. He wrote: "Although Mexico succeeded in challenging the first two of the Tribunal's findings of breaches of Articles 1105 and 1110, it was not successful on the remaining points. Accordingly, the Award should not be set aside in its entirety."

WORST CASE SCENARIO

The most bizarre and outrageous example of corporate behaviour in attempting to use a disputes settlement provision to its own advantage occurred in Bolivia. In early 1999 the World Bank advised the mayor of Cochabamba that financing for its water system was completely dependent on privatization. When a study showed that the project would not be profitable, the Bank proceeded to fund it anyway. The chosen vehicle was Bechtel Corporation and the Bank insisted that water be priced in such a way that all costs would be covered and the company would receive a 16% return on its investment.

The price of water increased by as much as triple which meant some people were paying up to 20% of their income for water.

"In a scenario impossible to parody, people not even hooked up to the system were told that they would have to put meters on their private wells and pay Bechtel for the water they drew. The resulting citizens' revolt shook the Bolivian government. It led to a week of protests, general strikes, and highway blockages which brought major areas of the country to a virtual standstill. The government caved in and told Bechtel to leave. The privatization was reversed and the water system handed over to the town."[5]

The company, however, had guessed what might happen. It took the precaution of moving its holding company from the Cayman Islands to Holland because it knew that Bolivia and Holland had a bilateral treaty with investment protection provisions not unlike Chapter 11 of NAFTA. This was the licence Bechtel needed to sue Bolivia for US$40 million in respect of a project which should never have been approved at the outset and probably wouldn't have been if it had not been for the pressure from the World Bank.

THE MULTILATERAL AGREEMENT ON INVESTMENT

When the Trilats and their colleagues achieved such splendid success with the FTA and NAFTA they decided to extend their power and influence on a much wider scale.

They supported Bilateral Investment Treaties (BITS) between countries and there are now more than 1,500 of those. But why do something piecemeal when it would be so much simpler to blanket most of the world in one grand treaty.

So an attempt was made to negotiate a multilateral agreement under the WTO which would have captured over 120 countries in one single net. Unfortunately for the globalizers, some of the Third World countries, including Brazil and India, balked at the thought of giving up so much sovereignty. So the whole project was aborted.

But the Trilats never give up. They want an "Empire" far vaster than the British Empire of the early part of the 20th century, which boasted that it was an "Empire" on which the sun never set. So they decided on a new tactic. They would abandon the WTO temporarily in favour of a Multilateral Agreement on Investment (MAI) which would be restricted to the 29 countries of the OECD, which just happens to include most of the wealthiest nations on earth.

The strategy was straight-forward. The OECD countries would negotiate a gold-plated investment agreement even more favourable to corporations than NAFTA. Once approved, the other countries of the world would be encouraged to adhere to the treaty under the largely unspoken threat that if they refused they could never expect to benefit from direct foreign investment from any of the major powers. The MAI, then, would provide the world with a far more investor-friendly treaty than anything that could be achieved under the WTO.

The plan almost worked. It was negotiated in near secrecy for two years before it became public knowledge. One of the Canadian negotiators denies the secrecy aspect by pointing to press releases put out by the Federal Department of Trade – press releases, I might add, that were ignored by the press and unknown to the public.

In any event, negotiations had been ongoing for about two years when I first heard of the infamous MAI at the time of the 1997 Canadian federal election. When I raised the subject at an all-candidates meeting none of the other candidates, including the incumbent member of parliament, had ever heard of it. My colleagues reported a similar experience.

Equally telling, in the course of a magazine interview early in the 1997 campaign, I told the reporter of my concerns about the MAI and what I considered to be its unacceptable consequences for Canada and other countries. She phoned back later to tell me that in the course of verifying my story she had called the Prime Minister's office for additional information – only to be told they had never heard of the MAI – which was interesting but not surprising.

After the election I took time off to write a book entitled *The Evil Empire: Globalization's Darker Side*, and then took two years off to criss-cross the country trying to raise the public awareness. A team effort including Council of Canadians Volunteer National Chairperson, Maude Barlow, Polaris Institute's Executive Director, Tony Clarke, and Citizens Concerned About Free Trade's, David Orchard, and others, did raise awareness. Internet connections were established with like-minded citizens in many OECD countries and progress was made but it still appeared we would lose because many countries, including Canada, were prepared to sign.

In the end, it was the French government, under tremendous pressure from an aroused electorate, which scuttled the deal because they feared losing control of their cultural sovereignty. So three cheers for the French for killing the MAI. It was a temporary victory but a victory nonetheless.

THE FREE TRADE AREA OF THE AMERICAS

The Free Trade Area of the Americas (FTAA) was an initiative of U.S. President Bill Clinton, himself a member of the Trilateral Commission. The project was launched at the first Summit of the Americas in Miami, Florida, in 1994. It was the second Summit in Santiago, Chile, in 1998, however, where the process really took off. Nine sectoral negotiating groups were established to propose a framework to regulate trade, investment, services, government procurement, agriculture, rules for settling disputes and intellectual property, amongst others. They were charged with preparing positions for presentation to the thirty-four leaders of the American States when they met in Québec City, April 21, 2001.

The fact that the leaders had to meet in what can best be described as a walled fortress, protected by thousands of police and soldiers, says something about the lack of universal approval of what was going on inside. A number of journalists, including the much respected Tony Westell, asked rhetorically, "who elected the protestors"[6] – as if the fact that we were not elected somehow diminished our rights as citizens. Unfortunately, the people who have been anaesthetized by the conventional wisdom have failed to understand what the fuss is all about.

In a word, it is a protest against a putsch. We are resisting the bloodless coup taking place worldwide – a coup that is ending the self-government for which men and women fought and died and replacing it with a kind of feudalism where the Lords and Ladies of Industry and Banking enjoy all the benefits of power and wealth while the majority must be content with the crumbs from their tables.

Democratic governments have legislated minimum wages, holidays with pay, maternity leave, public health care, public education and minimum universal retirement benefits. These things cost money that has to be raised by taxes. Trilats, however, don't like paying taxes – especially at the level required in most democracies.

So they are re-engineering the world in a way that allows them to set the rules, rather than the politicians. They want to have the freedom to move production to places where wages are low, there is no holiday pay, no sick leave, no maternity leave, no retirement benefits and minimum or non-existent safety and environmental standards. Instead of practising the Golden Rule, the New World Order assumes that those who have the gold make the rules.

Elite rule is as old as the world itself. Still many people hoped that we had become more civilized as the twentieth century ran its course. Instead we are seeing the demise of democracy and, for many of the world's masses, the end of hope as the disparity of income increases.

CHAPTER 4

THE ENFORCERS

" ... the culture of international economic policy in the world's most powerful democracy is not democratic."

Joseph Stiglitz
Former chief economist of the World Bank

It would be impossible for the Trilats to install the New World Order without the help of international institutions like the International Monetary Fund, the World Bank and the World Trade Organization which, collectively, act as "the Enforcers".

The International Monetary Fund (IMF) had its origin in the 1944 Bretton Woods agreement designed to stabilize the post-World War II international financial system. Its role was to provide member governments with short-term assistance when their foreign exchange reserves got too low as a result of propping up their currency to maintain the fixed exchange rate which had been agreed to.

Over the years, however, the system has changed. Fixed exchange rates have become the exception rather than the rule. Consequently, there is no compelling reason for central banks to deplete their reserves of foreign exchange in order to prop up the value of their own currency, except, perhaps, in the very short run to level out the peaks and valleys, although they sometimes do. They sell their U.S. dollars, euros, pounds, gold, or whatever they hold in their exchange reserves portfolio and spend the proceeds to buy their own currency, but they don't need to. Consequently there is no reason for an IMF to come to their rescue. The IMF has lost its original *raison d'être*.

But terminating organizations that have lost the rationale for their existence is ten times more difficult than launching a new one. Any bureaucracy will tend to find some excuse to keep going and the IMF is a first class example.

The IMF has become the lifeboat for international capital. This new lease on life was handed to it on a platter by Paul Volcker, Chairman of the U.S. Federal Reserve Board (FED) when he finally became aware that the worldwide recession he had precipitated in 1981-82 was about to collapse the world financial system.

In the 1970s much of the money that the industrial world had paid to Middle East oil producers was recycled through European banks as loans to Third World countries. These loans were made in U.S. dollars rather than being converted into pounds, marks or francs and became known as Eurodollars. For Third World countries it was like having a credit card with no credit limit, so eager borrowers took full advantage of it.

So did the banks, including American banks. Led by Citicorp Chairman Walter Wriston, the big international banks decided that lending vast amounts of money to Less Developed Countries (LDCs) was an easy way to get rich. Encouraged by the development of syndication and floating interest rates, which absolved them of interest rate risk, even small banks, with no expertise, climbed aboard the gravy train. Between 1970 and 1982, the profits on international operations (mostly LDC loans) of America's seven largest banks soared from 22% to 60% of total earnings.[1]

This was great business as long as interest rates were reasonable and the LDCs, as well as some of the more developed countries, could afford to pay the interest on the debt. When interest rates rose due to the FED's action, however, the bright sunshine gave way to gloom. Poland and Hungary had to refinance debt, Mexico teetered on the brink of default and one Latin American country after another found itself in financial difficulty. If markets had been allowed to operate as they should – those wonderfully effective markets that globalizers laud as the Road to Nirvana – virtually all of America's largest banks would have been bankrupt. But Paul Volcker, and other members of the central bankers' club, couldn't let that happen. So they performed a miracle.

Actually it wasn't a miracle! It was a wonderfully complicated web of intrigue and deceit; and anyone who has the stomach for it can read the gory details in *The Confidence Game: How Unelected Central Bankers Are Governing the Changed World Economy*, by Steven Solomon.[2] The bottom line was that the public was kept blissfully unaware that their banks were technically insolvent until the IMF could ride to the rescue with taxpayers' money.

This system of using taxpayers' money to save international capitalists worked so well that it was used again in the Mexican peso crisis, and later to bail out the international investors fleeing South-East Asia. The IMF does not ride to the rescue of the countries and people so negatively affected by the excesses of international capitalism. It is the foreign bankers and financial institutions that are the objects of its largesse. They are the ones who pick up their welfare cheques from the taxpayers of the world.

So if the IMF provides welfare for the rich and powerful, what does it do for the people of the poor nations that it bails out. In a word, it robs them of their freedom, self-respect and hope. Anyone brave or callous enough to tolerate bad news should read *The Globalisation of Poverty: Impacts of IMF and World Bank Reforms*, by Michel Chossudovsky,[3] professor of economics at the University of Ottawa, and *50 Years is Enough: The Case Against the World Bank and the International Monetary Fund*, edited by Kevin Danaher.[4]

The case histories are enough to bring tears to the eyes. Often devaluation of a nation's currency has been a pre-condition for IMF "help". Prices of food, drugs, fuel and other necessities rise dramatically and IMF "reforms" specifically prohibit domestic wage increases to compensate.

Recipient countries must open their borders to foreign products while domestic industries, unable to compete with imports, must be allowed to fail. Unemployment results. Direct foreign investment must be allowed and, on its own terms, rather than those of the host country. And, most important of all, the IMF prohibits the use of the country's central bank to help fund health care and education while encouraging the privatization of these services, or at least the imposition of user fees, which make it impossible for millions of children to attend school because their parents cannot afford even modest fees.

What I am describing, of course, is the end of democracy for that country. It is no longer able to make laws that are best suited to the health, welfare, education and business opportunities for its people. Instead, that country is subject to the arbitrary dictates of one of the worst international financial institutions on record which has become little more than an extension of U.S. foreign policy.

So, the IMF must be wound up. This conclusion has been reached by others including Former Secretary of the Treasury George Shultz, who told a committee of the U.S. Congress that the world financial system would be better off without the IMF, " ... because creditors would learn certain lessons. Don't loan money when there are questionable risks. Realize you'll be held accountable for your mistakes."[5] More surprisingly Milton Friedman endorsed this conclusion in an op-ed article in the *Wall Street Journal* of October 13, 1998. While not blaming private lenders for accepting the IMF's implicit offer of insurance against currency risk, he did blame the international agency for offering it.

The IMF must go! Not only that, all of the undemocratic conditions imposed on countries around the world should be annulled because they were imposed when those countries were in a state of duress.

THE WORLD BANK

When I began to write another book, *Stop: Think*, which includes entire chapters on the operations of the IMF and the World Bank, my pre-conceived position was a product of the conventional wisdom calling for greater concern for the poor, for women, greater transparency and other changes to increase both its popularity and its effectiveness. A little independent research led me to a different conclusion.

Like the IMF, the International Bank for Reconstruction and Development (IBRD), which is now universally known as the World Bank, was a product of the Bretton Woods agreement of 1944. Its initial objects were clear and admirable. It was not intended to compete with private banks but would guarantee their loans. There was little demand, however, because private banks were reluctant to make overseas loans and the Bank soon found it could make loans at lower interest rates on its own account once it had convinced Wall Street and the financial world that its bonds, guaranteed by the most powerful countries, were a safe and good investment.

For a balanced view of World Bank "success" you can read *The World Bank: Its First Half Century*,[6] by Devesh Kapur, John P. Lewis and Richard Webb, which is more or less the official view; and then *Masters of Illusion: The World Bank and the Poverty of Nations*,[7] a brilliantly written and extremely well documented exposé by Catherine Caufield; as well as the two books mentioned above in reference to the IMF. The four provide a pretty good overview of the Bank's activity.

The Bank literally changed the face of the Third World with its highways, railways, ports, mines, factories and dams – especially dams. It appears to have had a propensity to finance dams with little regard for the social or environmental consequences. That was due to the fact that the decisions were made by people who had little, if any, knowledge of the history, geography, climate or culture of the areas and people being affected. It was primarily a numbers game, played by economists whose mandate was to lend money for big projects.

It was the genesis of what has become a world disaster. When New York investment banker George Woods

succeeded Eugene Black as president of the Bank, he
discovered that Third World countries were taking on debt
faster than they could cope. Their foreign debt was growing
three times as fast as their economies. So Woods asked
Lester B. "Mike" Pearson, who had just retired as Canada's
prime minister, to head a high-level international commission
to study, among other things, the debt burden of developing
countries.

The commission report, "Partners in Development",
released in 1969, concluded that the rate of increase in Third
World debt had been explosive and could not be maintained.
A straight line projection showed that if borrowing continued
at then existing levels, by 1977 South Asia would be spending
all its new foreign loans to service existing debt; Africa's
debt service payments would be 120% of new borrowing and
Latin America's would be 130%,[8] and don't forget, that was
at a time when interest rates were still low.

The report should have set off alarm bells but, like
other big bureaucracies, the Bank simply applied greater
ingenuity in order to justify its continued existence. Loan
repayments were re-scheduled and the reasons for loans
extended in order to assist Third World countries to adjust
their economies to the Western model. Woods moved away
from the near-exclusive infrastructure funding of his
predecessors, to include social lending on the assumption that
it would increase growth and consequently the credit
worthiness of the borrower. It was a fond hope which was
destined to fail.

The situation went from bad to worse when Robert S.
McNamara, former U.S. Secretary of Defense, took over the
presidency from Woods. He decided the Bank should be
lending more, rather than less, and that it should invest more
in social services for the poor in the hope that the income
disparity could be narrowed.

Many of McNamara's reforms had the opposite effect
to the one intended. The Bank began to lend much more for
agriculture. The money, however, was not tailored to the
needs of small and subsistence farmers but to the wealthy two
percent who controlled three-quarters of the developing

world's farmland. In much of Latin America, for example, it was the big ranchers who were encouraged to clear rain forest to provide the ten acres or more of grazing land required for each animal.

The road to hell is paved with good intentions and the trip for the Bank was never-ending. Instead of its much touted "trickle-down" theory working to close the gap between rich and poor, that McNamara counted on when he made the loans to promote Western-style agribusiness, the disparity of income between classes increased. About the only thing rich and poor had in common was that their country was mortgaged to the hilt and the only way to avoid foreclosure was to negotiate new loans to pay the interest on the outstanding ones.

STRATEGIC ADJUSTMENT LOANS TO THE RESCUE?

Strategic Adjustment Loans (SALs) were not tied to any one specific project. Instead these new multi-million dollar loans were contingent on a Third World government's agreement to introduce drastic economic "reforms" in order to conform to the Washington consensus. "This included reducing the state's role in the economy, lowering barriers to imports, removing restrictions on foreign investments, eliminating subsidies for local industries, reducing spending for social welfare, cutting wages, devaluing the currency and emphasizing production for export rather than for local consumption."[9] In effect, the World Bank, like the IMF, was attempting to impose the neo-classical "Washington Consensus" on the vulnerable part of the world that comprised its client base.

Understandably, such a monumental interference in national sovereignty was enough to deter takers at the outset. But the Paul Volcker initiated debt crisis of the early 1980s made it increasingly impossible for Third World countries to service the huge loans made to them by Northern banks in the 1970s. One by one debtor countries capitulated. Additional private financing was not available without the World Bank imprimatur. So countries were driven to accept SALs. By

1985, 12 of the 15 top-priority debtors, including Argentina, Mexico and the Philippines were hooked. (Bank economists would probably say "rescued".)

"Over the next seven years, SALs proliferated as the economies of more and more Third World countries came under the surveillance and control of the Bank. About 187 SALs had been administered by the end of the decade, many of them coordinated with equally stringent standby programs administered by the IMF. Whereas in the previous division of labour between the two institutions, the World Bank was supposed to promote growth and the IMF was supposed to monitor financial restraint, their roles now became indistinguishable. Both became the enforcers of the North's economic rollback strategy."[10]

The effects of this economic counter-revolution have been ghastly. "The average Gross National Product for nations in sub-Saharan Africa fell by 2.2 percent per year in the 1980s; by 1990, per capita income on the continent was back down to its level at the time of independence in the 1960s. A United Nations advisory group reported that throughout the continent 'health systems are collapsing for lack of medicines, schools have no books, and universities suffer from a debilitating lack of library and laboratory facilities.' Structural adjustment programs have also promoted massive environmental damage, as many African countries were forced to cut down forests rapidly and exploit other natural resources more intensively to gain the foreign exchange they needed to make mounting interest payments."[11]

Africa's unhappy experience was not unique, as Walden Bello points out: "Latin Americans regard the reverse financial flow from their continent as the 'worst plunder since Cortez' and refer to the 1980s as the 'lost decade'. Per capita income in 1990 was at virtually the same level as ten years earlier. Severe malnutrition stalks the countryside, paving the way for the return of cholera, which people thought had been eradicated."[12]

WORLD BANK: "POLLUTE THE SOUTH"

Even a casual reading of the World Bank's history is enough to conclude that environmental concerns were never high on its list of priorities. Perhaps there were other urgent issues but there may have been an attitudinal problem, as well.

Lawrence Summers, who later became President Clinton's Secretary of the Treasury, was the World Bank's chief economist responsible for the 1992 *World Development Report,* devoted to the economics of the environment. He suggested that it made economic sense to shift polluting industries to the Third World countries. In a December 12, 1991 memo to senior World Bank staff he wrote: "Just between you and me, shouldn't the World Bank be encouraging more migration of the dirty industries to the LDCs?"

"Summers has justified his economic logic of increasing pollution in the Third World on the following grounds. Firstly, since wages are low in the Third World, economic costs of pollution arising from increased illness and death are lowest in the poorest countries. Summers thinks 'that the economic logic behind dumping a load of toxic waste in the lowest wage country is impeccable, and we should face up to that.'

"Secondly, since in large parts of the Third World pollution is still low, it makes economic sense to Summers to introduce pollution. 'I've always thought,' he says, that 'under-populated countries in Africa are vastly under-polluted; their air quality is probably vastly inefficiently low compared to Los Angeles or Mexico City.'

"Finally, since the poor are poor, they cannot possibly worry about environmental problems. 'The concern over an agent that causes a one-in-a million change in the odds of prostate cancer is obviously going to be much higher in a country where people survive to get prostate cancer than in a country where under-five mortality is 200 per thousand.'"[13]

The World Bank apologized for Summers' memo but the record shows that it has, in fact, been financing pollution-intensive industries in the Third World. It has funded steel plants, and pesticides and chemical fertilizer producers, for example. In addition, the use of the dangerous chemical, Agent Orange, was authorized to defoliate part of the Amazon basin for a dam of doubtful necessity.

The World Bank has demonstrated a classic disregard for environmental concerns, contributed mightily to the debt crisis in Third World countries, deprived these countries of their freedom of democratic action and has become, along with its sister organization the IMF, little more than an enforcer for the Northern industrialists and bankers who are systematically usurping the power of nation states.

To suggest that the World Bank can be reformed is naïve. Its collective mind-set is too close to the economics of Lawrence Summers. So it must be wound up. In the context of other reforms I will be suggesting it will no longer be needed. So it must go! Or, at the very least, it should be converted from a bank to a world relief agency so that it could really help people in need.

THE WORLD TRADE ORGANIZATION

The WTO, about which much more will be said in the next chapter, is the final link in the "unholy trinity". The cancerous outgrowth from what was once a respectable trading agreement is, in cooperation with the IMF and the World Bank, snuffing out rule of, by and for the people all around the globe. A noble experiment in popular democracy is coming to an end.

CHAPTER 5

THE DEATH OF DEMOCRACY

"Many forms of Government have been tried, and will be tried in this world of sin and woe. No one pretends that democracy is perfect or all-wise. Indeed it has been said that democracy is the 'worst' form of Government except all those others that have been tried from time to time."

Winston Churchill

The World Trade Organization (WTO) rings in the effective end of democracy and the establishment of a New World Order where commerce reigns and national governments are little more than rubber stamps providing legislative legitimacy to WTO rulings.

The WTO was established in 1995 as an outgrowth of the General Agreement on Tariffs and Trade, an organization which had been quite successful in negotiating rules for "Fair Trade" as opposed to the current push for "Free Trade", which is a horse of quite a different colour. At least one Canadian, Professor John Kirten, of the University of Toronto, claims that the WTO was a Canadian idea. When I heard him make that claim during the question period following a panel discussion at the St. Lawrence Centre, in Toronto, I had an almost irresistible urge to yell out, "shame on us". Fortunately my reticence prevailed. Since then, I have discovered, his claim is unlikely to be true.

Almost certainly the WTO came into being as a result of pressure from the United States which is the principal beneficiary, as the *Ecologist* stated in 1993. "Just as it was the U.S. which blocked the founding of the International Trade Organization (ITO) in 1948, when it felt that this would not serve its position of overwhelming dominance in the post-war world, so it was the U.S. that became the dominant lobbyist for the comprehensive Uruguay Round and the founding of the WTO in the late-eighties and early-nineties when it felt that more competitive global conditions had created a situation where its corporate interests now demanded an opposite stance.

"Just as it was the U.S.' threat in the 1950s to leave GATT if it was not allowed to maintain protective mechanisms for milk and other agricultural products that led to agricultural trade's exemption from GATT rules, so was it U.S. pressure that brought agriculture into the GATT-WTO system in 1995. And the reason for Washington's change of mind was articulated quite candidly by then U.S. Agriculture Secretary John Block at the start of the Uruguay Round negotiations in 1986: [The] idea that developing countries should feed themselves is an anachronism from a bygone era. They could better ensure their food security by relying on U.S. agricultural products, which are available, in most cases at much lower cost."[1] As Walden Bello observed, Washington, of course, did not just have developing country markets in mind, but also Japan, South Korea, and the European Union.[2]

My, what a part expediency plays in trade negotiations which are "sold" on the basis of the larger public benefit. The U.S. conversion to a policy of a single world market in agriculture just happens to coincide with the emergence of giant U.S. agribusinesses hell-bent on monopolizing the production of seed and food on a global basis.

How dependence on U.S. food suppliers "would better ensure [the] food security" of either developing or developed countries I cannot imagine. Where would developing countries get the U.S. dollars to pay for their food? It is a problem the Haitians already understand. Forced to open their borders to American produce, they have been inundated by the dark meat from American chickens because dark meat is not popular in the U.S. The imports have virtually destroyed the Haitians' poultry business, which was one of their few successful agricultural industries.

Japan would be reluctant to let the WTO run world agriculture for a different reason. It is genuinely concerned about its food supply in case of emergency and doesn't want to be in the position where it could be starved into submission. To put this concern in perspective, imagine what the U.S. might do if it found that all of its steel mills were forced to close because steel could be produced so much more cheaply in Third World countries? The U.S., of course, would invoke its general exemption for reasons of "national security."

Agriculture is not the only area of jurisdictional concern, but it is one of the most important. Most Americans resent what their giant agribusinesses are doing to their family farms and rural communities. But Monsanto, Cargill and Archer Daniels Midland have the big bucks which means the politicians are in their pockets. When they attempt to foist the same lack of choice on the world, all caring people should take serious notice.

The kind of open world agriculture now being negotiated under the WTO will mean that Canada will be unable to save what remains of our family farms and rural communities, even if we want to. The power of the transnationals would seal our fate. This, in my opinion, will be a terrible tragedy.

You may have noted, as I did, that Canadian Agriculture Minister Lyle Vanclief says he'll "go to the wall" to protect poultry, dairy and egg industries.[3] But that is just hogwash, if you'll pardon the expression. Either Vanclief is too naïve to be minister, or he is deliberately deceiving Canadians in support of the government's efforts to "sell" the idea of giving up even more sovereignty. Vanclief will go to the wall for farmers the same way Culture Minister Sheila Copps went to the wall for Canadian magazine publishers, only to have the WTO drop the wall on top of her.

CAPITALIST TOTALITARIANISM

Supporters of "Free Trade" didn't understand what the Seattle protest against the 2000 Millennium Round of WTO negotiations was all about. Various epithets including "riff-raff," "trouble-makers," and "rabble-rousers" were applied. At the Québec Summit in April, 2001, Prime Minister Jean Chrétien referred to protesters as like going for a picnic – a rah, rah.

In the event, a few sticks and stones were thrown at the police but whether this was by anarchists or "agent-provocateurs" is not absolutely certain. But it did give the press licence to paint all participants with one broad brush. Unfortunately, that superficial analysis is not only wrong but dangerous. This is not a fight between capitalism and socialism! In reality, it is a fight between democracy and totalitarianism! It is a fight against the kind of unfettered capitalism which the Hungarian-born U.S. financier George Soros says has "replaced fascism and communism as the greatest threat to open societies." In fact, open societies are becoming a thing of the past.

Protesters have been criticized because they are unelected, whereas the politicians who are doing the deals, are elected. This is another case of something being technically true while still being a terrible distortion of reality. Increasingly political leaders are "bought" by the elite groups who stand to benefit most from globalization. They get elected because anyone promoting a view contrary to that of the world elite wouldn't be able to raise enough money to buy their first TV ad.

Any political party that shows any potential for winning an election is blessed with corporate benevolence. This way is doesn't matter very much who wins. Once elected, the "indentured" politicians dutifully push the global agenda even if it means using the army and police forces, paid for with taxes from everyone including protesters, to achieve the desired result with the aid of barb-wire fences, pepper spray, tear gas and rubber bullets.

These are the tactics being used against people who are increasingly concerned and resentful when they begin to understand how much decision-making power has been transferred to the World Trade Organization and other international bodies. Now, slowly, comes the awful realization that the worst is yet to come.

Renato Ruggiero, former secretary general of the WTO, in an exuberant mood proudly proclaimed: "What we are doing is establishing a new world government." He changed his line when he was reminded that it wasn't politically correct to blurt out the truth. That doesn't fit the power brokers' strategy which is to create a *de facto* world government and then present it as a *fait accompli.*

Ruggiero's successor, Mike Moore, former New Zealand prime minister, is more diplomatic in his language but no less committed. He says that the protesters lack focus and don't have a clear understanding of what world organizations like the WTO, IMF and World Bank are trying to achieve. He is dead wrong! Every time someone takes the time to learn what these organizations are really up to, they become a protester.

Moore, like most politicians dedicated to a cause, is a master propagandist. "As you know, we're an intergovernmental organization," he said. "You have to be elected [and] represent a government to sit at the table."[4] He admits, however, that WTO members are split over the issue of how best to contain violent protests, such as the one in Seattle, while still including so-called "civil society" in an efficient and meaningful way. In the WTO's discussions, Canada and its allies, mainly other industrialized countries, are lining up against more fragile democracies, which are often developing countries.

That is the great divide in globalization. The Trilateral Commission's principal thrust is to maintain the dominion of the industrialized North over the poor and struggling South. The rules are designed to favour the powerful industrialized countries at the expense of the weak. And all of this is happening under the aegis of so-called "democratic" governments.

I don't remember voting for Canada to become part of the WTO. I don't remember voting for a new world government to exercise the most important powers previously exercised by Ottawa and the provinces. I didn't even know Canada was part of the WTO until long after the event, and I follow this kind of development more closely than many of my friends and relatives. Our birthright has been given away without our advice and consent, and now we learn that the worst is yet to come. Based on WTO decisions to date, we should all be taking to the street in protest.

WTO DECISIONS

One of the first decisions against Canada, and one of the ones that bothered me most was to deny Canada the right to penalize advertisers in split-run American magazines. This kind of protectionism on our part was absolutely justified and without it magazines like *Maclean's* might not have survived.

U.S. split-runs are one of the most blatant forms of dumping imaginable. The editorial content, which is primarily American or written from an American perspective, is paid for by the U.S. version of the magazine. The split-run starts with the advantage of a zero cost base for editorial content and production economies with which to skim off the cream of Canadian magazine advertising. It is a form of dumping that wouldn't be tolerated by the U.S. for one minute if the shoe were on the other foot.

Yet the U.S. government, at the insistence of its loyal supporter Time Warner Inc., as it then was, goes to the WTO and gets a binding ruling that our Canadian law was illegal, and this from a three-person panel that wouldn't know the difference between *Time* and *Maclean's* magazines. This bit of arbitrary nonsense from the WTO will wind up costing Canadian taxpayers $125 to $150 million in annual subsidies if we want to keep any semblance of an indigenous magazine industry alive.

The WTO ruled that the European Union ban against North American cattle that had been fed bovine growth hormones was illegal, and gave Canada and the U.S.

permission to slap $174 million in retaliatory tariffs on European imports. The case may be settled by the E.U. allowing increased quotas for non-hormone beef imports[5] but the principle involved of substituting arbitrary "wisdom" of WTO bureaucrats for E.U. wisdom and consumer preference is fundamental.

The WTO ruled that the Canada-U.S. Auto Pact was illegal, a sobering decision for all Canadians. We should remind ourselves that without the Auto Pact, a highly protectionist measure put in place before the FTA was signed, much of the limited success attributed to that accord by its boosters would not have occurred. This is another way of saying that if the globalized world of the present and future had been in place a decade or so earlier, the consequences would have been even more disastrous for us.

Until recently, every WTO decision pitting commerce against the environment had been decided in favour of commerce. The U.S. was told it could not ban the import of tuna caught in nets that drown sea turtles. It was also told it could not ban gasoline from Venezuela that contained a level of impurities far higher than U.S. standards allowed.

The first break in this tradition was a case lost by Canada. We had argued that France had no right to prevent imports of chrysolite asbestos under the guise of protecting public health. In a landmark decision the WTO panel rejected Canadian arguments and validated the French import ban.

One of the most far-reaching decisions was one requiring Canada to amend its patent law to correspond to U.S. law. Here again is an indication of the trend to world hegemony. The U.S. sets the standards, and the rest of the world has to get in line. In any event, it is a decision which will cost Canadians dearly as taxpayers will have to shell out about $200 million additional to pay for drugs at a time when our health care system is already in crisis due to under-funding.

A decision that upset Americans was a panel finding that the billions of dollars worth of tax benefits under the U.S. Foreign Sales Corporation legislation offended the WTO system of rules. Even business leaders who have been supportive of multilateralism were outraged and a resolution was presented to Congress calling for U.S. withdrawal from the WTO. There was no chance of it passing, however, because wiser heads would know that the U.S. is the principal beneficiary of that organization and it has to be prepared to take a few bumps from time to time.

Canada suffered a significant blow when the WTO deemed a $3-billion loan fund, controlled mainly by Canada's Minister of International Trade, to be illegal, at the same time that the world body condemned the Technology Partnerships, the federal government's foremost industrial development program. Both are considered to be subsidies.

These rulings underline the difficulty any world body has in establishing rules that apply fairly in all cases. Canadian officials claim that we do what we do because other countries have similar programs. But even if they didn't, it is difficult to achieve genuine equity. When Canada eliminated the Defence Research Board (DRB), in 1974, it virtually abandoned the kind of military research that inevitably produces subsidized civil spin-offs for industrial production. Meanwhile the U.S. spends billions in this area and the commercial benefits are enormous. They give U.S. industry a significant advantage in the marketplace, and yet this advantage is not considered to be a subsidy by the WTO. There is no real justice, just as there never will be a genuinely level playing field. The giants will always have the advantage.

EXPANDING THE WTO's POWER

The General Agreement on Trade in Services (GATS) is one of the many agreements that are administered by the World Trade Organization. The WTO describes the significance of this agreement as follows. "The GATS is the first multilateral agreement to provide legally enforceable rights to trade in all services. It has a built-in commitment to continuous liberalization through periodic negotiations. And it is the world's first multilateral agreement on investment, since it covers not just cross-border trade but every possible means of supplying a service, including the right to set up a commercial presence in the export market."[6]

Some of the activities on the WTO list of "services" that can potentially be opened up to foreign competition include:

- Medical and dental services, services provided by midwives, nurses, physiotherapists and paramedical personnel.
- Education – primary, secondary, tertiary and adult.
- Recreational, cultural and sports services, including entertainment, libraries, archives and museums.
- Publishing, printing, advertising.
- Environmental services including road construction and maintenance, rubbish collection, sewage disposal, water delivery, protection of the landscape and urban planning.

At the time of writing, the principal areas under negotiation are health care, education and intellectual property in addition to agriculture. What that really means is that the WTO will be given the right to amend and over-rule our laws in each of these areas. Decisions reached by unelected, unaccountable panels will supersede those of our elected representatives. And they call that democracy!

TRADE AND INDUSTRIALIZATION

In his magnificent paper entitled "Why Reform of the WTO is the Wrong Agenda," Dr. Walden Bello, executive director of Focus on the Global South, describes how the developing countries have lost the right to use trade policy to help industrialize their countries. In signing on to the WTO, under U.S. pressure, and being subject to its Trade-Related Investment Measures (TRIMs) and Trade-Related Intellectual Property Rights (TRIPs), they have lost the leverage they previously had with foreign investors. (For anyone really interested in how the WTO affects poorer countries, please read his paper in full. www.focusweb.org/publications/2000)

Bello cites the contrast between the old rules and the new. "The U.S. industrialized, to a great extent, by using but paying very little for British manufacturing innovations, as did the Germans. Japan industrialized by liberally borrowing U.S. technological innovations, but barely compensating the Americans for this. And the Koreans industrialized by copying quite liberally, and with little payment, U.S. and Japanese product and process technologies.

"But what is 'technological diffusion' from the perspective of the late industrializer, is 'piracy' from that of the industrial leader. The TRIPs regime takes the side of the latter and makes the process of industrialization by imitation much more difficult from here on. It represents what the United Nations Conference on Trade and Development (UNCTAD) describes as a premature strengthening of the intellectual property system ..."[7]

But that is really what globalization is all about. The United States, Europe and Japan want to keep the South, and smaller countries everywhere, in their place. The Trilats have long been determined that the South would be a safe, reliable source of raw materials and a market for industrial products from the North. But industrial competitors? Not if the WTO can prevent it!

A RULES-BASED SYSTEM

Whenever Sylvia Ostry, one of Canada's principal negotiators at the Uruguay Round of GATT negotiations, is cornered on the subject of where the WTO is taking us, and the extent of sovereignty we are losing, she replies: "Well, you have to have a rules-based trading system." It sounds so reasonable that one hesitates to quarrel. But sometimes one must probe beneath the superficialities and ask "whose rules?" And "who are the chief beneficiaries?"

It is a fact that the rules under which the WTO operates were written by, or with direct input from, the chief executive officers of some of the largest transnational corporations in the world. Who benefits most? Take a guess. You can eliminate the poor of the world. Then you can eliminate the poor countries of the world, where most of the people live. Next, you can cross off smaller branch plant economies like Canada, for example. Finally you can eliminate environmentalists and humanitarians who are concerned about the survival of the planet and some reasonable justice for all its inhabitants.

Who is left? Only the transnational corporations and international banks situated in the United States, Japan, Germany, the United Kingdom, and France. The result is not surprising, but this is what Trilateralism means.

The WTO rules are fundamentally flawed in two ways. First, their bias toward commerce and the interests of big, monopolistic business. Second, and equally profound, the rules, with minor exceptions are universal and global in their application. Everyone gets in the ring with the big guy and gets the stuffing knocked out of him.

That is the rule! And nowhere is this of greater significance than in the realm of international finance. Big banks call the shots! So it is important to know where they get the money to rule the world.

CHAPTER 6

THE ROOT OF ALL EVIL

"The process by which banks create money is so simple the mind is repelled. Where something so important is involved, a deeper mystery seems only decent."

J.K. Galbraith[1]

The love of money may indeed be the root of all evil but it is the lack of understanding of what it is and where it comes from that has caused so much chaos and distress. The most powerful tool in the economic toolbox is simply not understood by the people who wield the levers of power.

This became painfully obvious a few years ago when I was writing a book on the subject. I asked more than a hundred well-educated people where money comes from and not one of the hundred knew the answer. None had what you could call a working knowledge of the monetary system. Yet these same people give governments economic advice.

Some were people whose names you might recognize. Paul Godfrey, who was the publisher of the *Toronto Sun;*[2] Peter Cook, well-known financial columnist for the *Globe and Mail;*[3] his boss, at the time, William Thorsell, then editor in chief;[4] and Diane Francis, then editor of the *Financial Post.*[5] There were others who are just as well known.

The problem is, as Galbraith pointed out, that the means by which money is created is so simple people won't believe it. During the 1997 federal election campaign, when the fledgling Canadian Action Party was promoting the idea of using the Bank of Canada to help finance essential public services, rather than continue as an agency responsible for the partial destruction of just about everything which had made Canada a progressive, exciting and respected middle power, many journalists scoffed. "This is the party that wants to print money", they said, with sarcasm thick enough to cut. Some even dramatized their disdain by showing printing presses spewing out a stack of bills.

If their minds were as agile as their tongues they would know that, with the exception of a few coins that are minted, all money is printed. A small amount, about 5%, is printed on fine paper by the Bank of Canada. This is the kind of money you carry in your purse or pocketbook in case you need cash for any reason. It is Canada's legal tender.

All of the rest of our "money" is printed by the private banks on computer paper, or simply stored in their computers. The term printing money is often used in the pejorative so if you would be more comfortable with "creating money" or "manufacturing money" that is fine with me – printing, creating or manufacturing, it's all the same.

Graham Towers, the first and unquestionably the brightest of Bank of Canada governors, said: "Banks manufacture money the same way that steel companies manufacture steel, that is their business." He made no attempt to disguise the nature of money. "It is nothing but a book entry; that is all it is," he said. If he were alive today he would say: "Money is nothing but a computer entry; that is all it is."

HOW BANKS CREATE MONEY

The most important myth that banks attempt to perpetuate is that they are simply financial intermediaries and only lend depositors' money. That is far from the whole truth. They are financial intermediaries, but that isn't all. They also create new money every time they make a new loan – or destroy money when they cancel one. The system works this way:

A builder needs to borrow $200,000 to build a house. Once he has provided the bank with sufficient collateral – it could be a mortgage on another house – a note will be signed and, presto, $200,000 will be posted to his account. It is a kind of double-entry bookkeeping where the note becomes an asset on the bank's books and the new deposit becomes a liability.

The important point, however, is that just seconds earlier the new money did not exist. It was created out of thin air based on nothing more than a small capital reserve as required by the Bank Act. Canadian banks create billions of dollars this way every year. Some of it is used creatively to finance new businesses or to permit others to expand. This is positive lending which helps the real economy to grow.

Increasingly, however, banks have been creating money for preferred customers to buy stocks on margin – a practice under which people borrow a substantial proportion of what they pay for stocks, bonds or shares in mutual funds. This is highly questionable lending because the banks are diluting the money supply for everyone without any corresponding growth in the output of goods and services in the real economy.

MONEY AND INFLATION

It makes a difference what newly printed money is used for because some purposes are inflationary and some are not. An analogy I like is that of Irish stew.

Consider the modern industrial economy as something like a rich, satisfying Irish stew containing tempting chunks of meat and an almost infinite variety of vegetables. If new bits of meat and more vegetables are added at the same rate that water is added, the consistency of the stew remains the same. If too much water is added in relation to the other ingredients the soup is thinner, or, in real life, inflation occurs.

So two things are key. The total amount of water that is added, and whether or not it is matched by the other ingredients. Obviously if the proportion of water is increased this will be inflationary. That is a matter of increasing concern in recent years as banks have moved from retail to wholesale operation. Less of their new lending has been directed at the real economy and much more to the paper economy.

THE BANKING SCAM

Banking is an ancient scam which probably had its origin in Babylon.[6] My review, however, will start with the London goldsmiths in the latter half of the 17th century. Until 1640 it was the custom for wealthy merchants to keep their excess cash – gold and silver – in the Mint at the Tower of London for safe-keeping. In that year King Charles I seized the privately-owned money and destroyed the Mint's reputation as a safe place. This action forced merchants and traders to seek alternatives and, subsequently, to store their excess money with the goldsmiths of Lombard Street who had already built strong fire-proof boxes for the storage of their own valuables.[7]

The goldsmiths accepted gold and silver deposits for which they issued receipts which were redeemable on demand. These receipts were passed from hand to hand and were known as goldsmiths' notes, the predecessors of banknotes. The goldsmiths paid interest of 5 percent on their customers' deposits and then lent the money to their more needy customers at exorbitant rates becoming, in fact, pawnbrokers who advanced money against the collateral of valuable property.[8] They also learned that it was possible to make loans in excess of the gold actually held in their vaults because only a small fraction of their depositors attempted to convert their receipts into gold at any one time. It was a practice that later became known as the fractional reserve system, the practice of lending "money" that doesn't really exist. This practice was to become the most profitable scam in the history of mankind. It was also the quicksand on which the Bank of England was subsequently founded in 1694 – a little more than three hundred years ago.

THE BANK OF ENGLAND SCAM

The Bank of England was conceived as the solution to a dilemma. King William's War, 1688-1697, had been extremely costly and this resulted in much of England's gold and silver going to the continent in payment of debt. As a result, the money supply was sorely depleted and something had to be done to keep the wheels of commerce turning. Someone got the bright idea that establishing a bank might help fill the void.

At the time the Bank was chartered, the scheme involved an initial subscription of £1,200,000 in gold and silver which would be lent to the government at 8 percent. That seems fair enough, although the interest rate was more than ample for a government-guaranteed investment. It was only the beginning, however, because in addition to a £4,000 management fee, the Bank of England was granted an advantage only available to banks and bankers. It was granted authority to issue "banknotes" in an amount equal to its capital and lend the notes into circulation. This was not the first case of paper money issued by private banks in the modern era but it was the first of great and lasting significance in the English-speaking world.[9]

BANKS ARE NEVER SATISFIED!

In the slightly over 300 years since the Bank of England began with a leverage of two-to-one (in effect, lending the same money twice), the deal has been sweetened many times. In the early years of the 20th century, federally chartered U.S. banks were required to have a gold reserve of 25 percent, that is, banks could lend the same money four times. State chartered banks were subject to less restraint and there were some shocking examples of excess.

With the introduction of Central Banks, the Federal Reserve System in the U.S. and the Bank of Canada north of the border, the system changed in form though not in substance. Banknotes issued by private banks were phased out and replaced by a uniform, legal tender, currency. In the

U.S., Federal Reserve Notes became predominant, while in Canada, the Bank of Canada was given a monopoly on the creation of legal tender paper money. In the process, banks were required to keep cash, legal tender, reserves against deposits instead of gold.

Consequently, in Canada, when I was younger, the cash reserve requirement for banks was 8% which allowed them to lend the same money 12½ times. Today the cash reserve requirement in the U.S. is 3% for current accounts, 0% for savings accounts and 0% for Eurodollar accounts. In Canada, the reserve requirement is 0%, period! You are lucky if your bank has a cent, or a cent-and-a-half, in cash, for every dollar you think you have in the bank. The only reason they can get away with this is the time-honoured one of knowing from experience that only a handful of depositors are likely to ask for cash at any one time. If for any reason depositors' confidence was shaken, and they began a "run" on the bank, they would be out of luck because their "money" doesn't exist in real form. Their only hope would be a massive intervention by the Bank of Canada to monetize (print legal tender money to buy) the bonds and other assets held by the banks.

It was Prime Minister Brian Mulroney who eliminated the requirement for Canadian banks to hold cash reserves. The Bank Act of 1991 phased them out. This was a gift worth several billion dollars a year to the banks, at taxpayers expense. They were allowed to spend their reserves to purchase bonds and treasury bills on which we, the tax-payers, pay several billions a year in extra interest payments.

In lieu of cash reserves, Canadian banks are not allowed to own assets in excess of twenty times their paid up capital. At least that is what the law says, although anyone who examines the banks' annual statements will know that they have found ingenious means of stretching that limit. The new system, which is called "capital adequacy," is quite inferior to the necessity for cash reserves. It is a system which the Bank for International Settlements (BIS), with its headquarters in Basle, Switzerland, has foist upon an unsuspecting world. It is all part of the plan to switch the world banking system to 0% reserves in accord with the theories of Professor Milton Friedman and his colleagues, formerly of the University of Chicago.

Of Professor Friedman's several ideas none has greater potential for disaster than his support for deregulation of financial institutions, and getting governments out of the money-creation function. Accepting the notion of 0% cash reserves for deposit-taking institutions, thereby giving back to the private banks their virtual monopoly to create money, will likely prove to be his greatest and most tragic legacy.

It is curious that Friedman would recommend 0% reserves when he claims to believe that 100% reserves, as recommended by his mentor, Lloyd W. Mints of the Chicago School of the 1930s, would be better.[10] His only explanation for jumping from 100% to 0% is politics. He has concluded that establishing a 100% reserve system is politically impossible whereas the adoption of the 0% system is politically feasible. He is right on that latter score as Canada has led the way in letting the banks get away with 0% reserves.

In addition to putting the money-creation function almost entirely in private hands, which history has demonstrated to be an unworkable system, "capital adequacy" has the additional disadvantage of being a "risk-weighted" system. Under the BIS formula, adopted by the Canadian parliament, it can be more advantageous for banks to buy government bonds than it is to make commercial loans. This is because business loans are considered "risky", and consequently must be backed by 8% of the banks' capital compared to a maximum of 5% for government bonds which are considered to be risk free – an assumption which, historically, is open to some question. It is the bias against the real, wealth-creating economy, however, that is of the greatest concern. The BIS has finally concluded that its original prescription was faulty and the whole question of risk weighting is under review at the time of writing.

Apart from the utter hopelessness of a money-creation system based entirely on debt, high bank leverage has been the intrinsic weakness of the capitalist system. When times are good, we allow the banks to blow up the money supply like a balloon. Then if inflation results, and central banks want to tighten the money supply, the leverage works in reverse – like a balloon with a pin stuck in it. It is no accident that there have been 45 recessions and depressions in the last 200 years. In my opinion, every one of them was due to the banking system and there is no hope for a recession-proof world economy until the system is changed and bank leverage reduced to something closer to that considered prudent for other businesses.

A FAULTY SYSTEM

The current monetary system is fundamentally flawed. Consider this proposition: If nearly all the new money created each year is created by private banks, which it is; and if all of that bank-created money is created as debt, on which interest has to be paid, which is the case; and if no one creates any money with which to pay that interest, which is the current situation; what do you have to do? The answer: You have to borrow the money with which to pay the interest on what you already owe, and go deeper and deeper into debt in the process.

Look around the world and see the accumulated debt in France, Germany, the U.K., Canada, the U.S. and other countries. This debt is not primarily due to profligate spending by successive generations of politicians, as some people insist; although I readily admit that there have been and always will be cases of waste and extravagance. The mountain of debt, worldwide, is the direct result of a monetary system where most of the money is created as debt.

Furthermore, there is no way, under the current system, that it can ever be repaid. The money necessary to do that does not exist. There may be some reshuffling of the debt. Indeed that is already happening. Instead of borrowing the money for new roads, bridges, sewers, waterworks, and an array of other infrastructure projects, governments are farming these works out to private enterprises which, in turn, will have to borrow the money to construct them. The amount of money that will have to be borrowed will not be less, and the cost will not be less because interest rates will be higher than those available to government. But the switch from public to private will provide a cosmetic "high" to those who work on the principle that debt which is out of sight, will be out of mind.

People who speak largely in terms of federal government debt as the principal economic problem have their heads in the sand. Net federal debt in Canada never exceeded $600 billion, whereas the total federal, provincial, municipal, corporate and private debt exceeds $1.8 trillion. That is almost twice as much as our Gross Domestic Product (GDP). Unfortunately the average interest rate on that debt is much greater than the growth rate of the economy. Consequently, the debt is growing faster than the economy and interest payments take a bigger and bigger bite out of our income.

Eventually the burden gets too great and we have a bit of a meltdown which we call a recession, when bankruptcies increase and some of the debt is written off. A by-product of this instability, of course, is waste. Every time the cycle turns down, human and economic resources are sacrificed. In a system geared to debt, an economy can only expand when someone – business individuals or governments – is prepared to borrow more and go deeper in debt. That is the only way that the money supply will increase and the economy grow.

It should be apparent that our present system of privately-created money is not sustainable. The only reason we survived so well in the early post-World War II years is because the money-creation function was shared with government. The Bank of Canada provided the federal government with significant sums of near-zero interest money which gave it some fiscal flexibility. In addition, interest rates in the 1950s and 1960s were low – about equal to the growth rate of the economy. Consequently total debt grew in proportion to the economy but the debt to GDP ratio held steady.

Actually it was the system of shared public/private money-creation which got us out of the Great Depression, helped finance World War II, helped pay for the post-war infrastructure including the St. Lawrence Seaway, the Trans-Canada Highway, our airport improvements and helped pay for the expansion of our social security system. This was the monetary system that gave us the best twenty-five years of the twentieth century. All of that changed in 1974 when the Bank of Canada adopted the economic ideas of Milton Friedman and his colleagues including privatized banking and volatile interest rates. It has been downhill ever since!

COUNTERFEIT MONEY

Bank-created money (BCM) has been called "credit money," "computer money" and "virtual money". If it were labelled more precisely, it would be called "counterfeit money", because that is what it really is. Of course there are two kinds of counterfeit money. There is the kind that some people print in their basements or workshops which looks like legal tender. When they attempt to buy something with it, and get caught, they go to jail. Then there is the other kind of counterfeit money printed by the banks, under licence from parliament, which comprises 95% of the total money supply. The people who print this kind of money on their computers usually wind up as Chair of the Board of Governors of universities, hospitals, and other public institutions and are awarded the Order of Canada for their efforts.

GOVERNMENT-CREATED MONEY IS ESSENTIAL

The patent to print money is the most valuable asset owned by the parliament and Government of Canada on behalf of the people of Canada. It is a total mystery why, in that case, parliament has granted licenses to private individuals without demanding a substantial royalty. In what other domain can you enjoy the use of a very valuable property and not pay rent?

Even worse, the banks charge the people for the use of their own patent. When the government needs a little money it goes, cap in hand, to the banks and says, "Please will you use the licence we have given you to print a little money for us?" "Of course we will pay you market rates of interest on the loan." Doesn't that strike you as more than a little silly?

There are six banks on the street, and you own one of them. Five of them want to charge you 6% interest whereas your own bank will lend it to you at 0% interest. You walk past your own bank and pay one or more of the others 6 percent. If you owned shares in a company where the Chief Executive Officer (CEO) and the Chief Financial Officer (CFO) were deliberately paying more than necessary to borrow money, and you found out about it, you would fire them. Yet that is exactly what the CEO of the country, Jean Chrétien, and the CFO, Paul Martin, have been doing and we, the beleaguered taxpayers say nothing. There is an old saying that people deserve the government they get!

Why is government-created money essential?

(a) It is essential because there is no other way to stop the growth of debt in Canada, and in the world, and to reduce the total debt to GDP ratio. It will also reduce the federal debt to GDP ratio.

(b) There is no other way that governments can have the fiscal flexibility to meet both the needs and demands of the electorate. They simply cannot raise enough money through conventional taxes alone. Most people think that taxes are presently too high. CEOs threaten to move their companies out of the country if taxes are not reduced. Some individual Canadians have left, or are considering leaving, due to the lure of lower taxes elsewhere. Yet, at the same time, they want more money spent on health care, education, environmental concerns, affordable housing, the arts, drug testing and a long list of other real concerns. There is absolutely no way of accommodating these seemingly conflicting concerns except through the use of significant amounts of government-created money.

(c) There is no other politically feasible way to pay off Third World debt and give the hundreds of millions of desperate people who live there a chance for a decent and rewarding life.

GOVERNMENT-CREATED MONEY IS NOT NEW

It is probably true that there is nothing new under the sun and certainly that is the case with government-created money (GCM). Consider the experience of the early English settlers in the New World. Few were independently wealthy and the colonies suffered a chronic and often acute shortage of gold and silver coins. To make matters worse, Britain routinely banned the export of silver and gold to the colonies because it was desperately required as a base for the expansion of the money supply in the mother country. Deprived of support from "mother" England, necessity became the mother of invention.[11]

In 1690, four years before the Bank of England was chartered, the Massachusetts Bay Colony issued its first colonial notes. This, according to one of my American friends, was a consequence of their part in King William's war. Soldiers had been dispatched to invade Canada on the promise that the French had lots of silver; "Beat 'em and get paid that way," is how he told the story. But Québec did not fall and the Yanks went back to Boston sore, mean and unpaid. Something had to be done, so the Massachusetts Bay Note, redeemable in gold "sometime" was born. "This was, if not the very first, one of the first cases of government-created paper money [fiat money] of the modern age."[12]

Early in the 18th century, in May 1723, Pennsylvania loaned into circulation, with real estate as security, notes to the amount of £15,000; and another £30,000 was issued in December. It was enacted that, "counterfeiters were to be punished by having both their 'ears cut off', being whipped on the 'back with thirty lashes well laid on', and fined or sold into servitude."[13] While the punishment for counterfeiters seems somewhat extreme by 20th century standards, the issue of notes accomplished its purpose and sparked a revival of the colony's economy. Ship-building prospered and both exports and imports increased markedly.[14]

The experiment was so successful that the number of notes in circulation was increased from £15,000 in early 1723, to £81,500 in 1754 – a growth rate during the thirty-one years of a modest 5.6 percent. Even Adam Smith, who was not a fan of government-created money, admitted that Pennsylvania's paper currency "is said never to have sunk below the value of the gold and silver which was current in the colony before the first issue of paper money."[15]

The Chinese had used paper money centuries earlier, but for our part of the world, as Curtis P. Nettles points out: "Paper currency issued under government auspices originated in the thirteen colonies; and during the 18th century they were the laboratories in which many currency experiments were performed."[16] There were no banks at that time in any of the thirteen colonies so all the paper money was created under the authority of the colonial legislatures. In all, there were about 250 separate issues of colonial notes between 1690 and 1775 and the system worked just fine when they avoided issuing too much or too little new money. It also had distinct advantages over bank or coin money. The legislature could spend, lend or transfer the money into circulation, while banks could only lend (or spend their interest earnings back into circulation) and the coin money was always leaving the colonies to pay for imports. Government-created money has the same advantage over bank-created money today that it had then.

Historians play down the role of money creation as a causal factor in bringing about the War for Independence. We are lead to believe that it was all about tea and taxes. But there were more important reasons, as James Ferguson explains, "[Benjamin] Franklin cited restrictions upon paper money as one of the main reasons for the alienation of the American provinces from the mother country."[17] This point of view was confirmed by William F. Hixson in *Triumph of the Bankers*. "To a significant extent, the war was fought over the right of the Colonists to create their own money supply. When the Continental Congress and the states brought forth large issues of their own legal-tender money in 1775, they committed acts so contrary to British laws governing the colonies and so contemptuous and insulting to British sovereignty as to make war inevitable."[18]

This was a clear case of the banks versus the people. When the colonists started to create their own money and London banks became aware of it, they realized that a vast new market for loans was being lost. Furthermore, they didn't want other parts of the world to adopt the same radical practice. So they persuaded the parliament at Westminster to pass a law prohibiting it. This meant that instead of looking after their own financial needs, the colonists had to borrow from the London banks and repay, principal and interest, in gold that they didn't have. This led inevitably to a bad recession and increased unemployment – a situation not too different from that existing in many parts of the world in 2001 – setting the stage for war.

VICTORY OF THE BANKERS

It was the Civil War in the United States that had the greatest impact on the system. Although Abraham Lincoln had not been a proponent of GCM, he certainly recognized its usefulness in time of emergency. In his December 1862 message to Congress, Lincoln made the following reference to the failure of the banks and the need for GCM. "The suspension of specie payments [their failure to provide gold or silver coins in exchange for their bank notes] by banks soon after the commencement of your last session, made large issues of United States Notes [greenbacks] unavoidable. In no other way could the payment of the troops, and the satisfaction of other just demands, be so economically or so well provided for. The judicious legislation of Congress, securing the receivability of theses notes for loans and internal duties, and making them a legal tender for other debts, has made them a universal currency; and has satisfied, partially, at least, and for the time, the long felt want of a uniform circulating medium, saving thereby to the people immense sums in discounts and exchanges."[19]

While the immediate need had been to meet the exigencies of war, President Lincoln had also recognized the long-standing necessity for a "universal" or national currency to replace the hodgepodge of bank notes existing at that time. One historian estimated that in 1860 there were "7,000 kinds of paper notes in circulation, not to mention 5,000 counterfeit issues."[20]

From the time greenbacks first came into circulation in 1862 they carried the words: "The United States of America will pay to the bearer five dollars ... payable at the United States Treasury." In fact, however, they were government-created inconvertible money until 1879 when they first became convertible into gold at face value. It will come as no surprise that this switch in policy was engineered by Hugh McCulloch, a former banker and gold monometallist who became secretary of the treasury in 1865. He sold bonds in exchange for greenbacks and then destroyed the greenbacks. In this way he managed to load the government up with debt for no good reason except to reinforce the concept of a bankers' monopoly to create money.

THE GUERNSEY EXPERIMENT

When skeptics ask for an example in real life where government-created money has been utilized consistently and effectively for an extended period it is only necessary to look at the history of the Isle of Guernsey, beginning in the early 19th century. At that time the island boasted natural beauty but little else. There was nothing to attract visitors or to keep residents from moving to the mainland. There was no trade nor hope of employment for the poor. The market was open and needed a cover and the shores were eroding due to the sorry state of the dykes. What to do? Why set up a committee, of course.

Finally, as Olive and Jan Grubiak report in *The GUERNSEY Experiment*, "after grave deliberation, the Committee reported in 1816 with this historic recommendation – that property should be acquired and a covered market erected; the expenses to be met by the Issue of States Notes to the value of £6000."[21]   The story, as related by the Grubiaks in their well documented pamphlet, is well worth reading for anyone interested in the subject.

The experiment had its ups and downs as the banks made a valiant, but in the end unsuccessful, effort to put an end to the practice. Consequently, it has persisted to this day with the result that the island has modern infrastructure, no unemployment to speak of, very low taxes and no debt. If you contrast this extremely successful policy with that of the United Kingdom with its enormous debt, and taxpayers still paying interest on money borrowed to fight the American colonists in the War for Independence more than 200 years ago, it will be hard to escape the conclusion that there is a better system and that we would be well advised to adopt it.

GCM – THE 50% SOLUTION

For several years I have been suggesting that the money-creation function be split 50/50 between government and private enterprise. I am often asked why? Why not recommend that cash reserve requirements be set at 100 percent of deposits as suggested by many monetary reformers including the original Chicago School of Simon, Mints and colleagues, Yale professor Irving Fisher and others including Milton Friedman, who still claims it is his preferred solution. In reply, I freely admit that the choice is an arbitrary one. It is the compromise that I believe is most likely to produce the fairest and most advantageous balance of power and benefit – just another way of saying the greatest good for the greatest number.

I can't say for certain if 40 percent would do, or if 60 percent would be better. Nor can anyone else because the system is far too complicated and it may take 10 or 20 years of experience to know if the 50/50 split will be sufficient. In any event, the 50 percent solution is much easier to defend than either the 100 percent solution or the zero percent solution, the choice of extremes that Milton Friedman prefers.

In the first case of 100 percent, one would be removing from the banks a very, very large proportion of their interest bearing assets. In my opinion this would be too disruptive. I don't mind seeing them scratch for a living, the way everyone else must, but I don't want to put them out of business altogether. The 50 percent solution allows them to survive and still prosper.

I am convinced that they have, in times past, and can in the future, play a useful role in the allocation of new money to productive enterprise. I suspect that there is as much cronyism as there would be if governments were involved but much of that should disappear if banks were forbidden to create money for buyouts, takeovers and mergers on the industrial side, and for financing the purchase of stocks and bonds on margin on the financial side. In any event, I am not willing to encourage government involvement in the direct allocation of credit – one point on which Milton Friedman and I agree.

The 50 percent solution would leave the banks enough elbow room to continue to be profitable. A bank economist who read *Stop: Think*, an earlier book on this subject, told me that the banks would be required to call their loans. In rebuttal, I took the most recent annual report of his bank and showed that his fear was unfounded. The bank would have to sell many of its stocks, bonds and other non-loan assets but it could achieve the 50 percent cash reserve level without calling any of its loans unless it chose to do so.

Furthermore, anyone who reads bank annual reports, as I do, will know that they now brag that traditional banking is becoming less important all the time as an increasing proportion of their revenue comes from service fees, underwriting, money management and the other financial services they provide. So there would be no need to dump bank shares if the 50 percent solution were imposed, even though the growth rate of their assets, and consequently profits, would be slowed. This would be partly offset by a reduction in the number of bad loans as the temptation to gamble was curbed.

THE INFLATION BUGBEAR

Whenever GCM is mentioned in polite circles you can expect the knee-jerk reaction, "It would be inflationary." This is a substitute for thinking on the part of economists and editorial writers who put it forward in all seriousness as a defense. As I have pointed out in reference to the early experiments by the American Colonies, and the long-time experience in Guernsey, this is not necessarily so. Still many people who should know better write off GCM on the basis of selective evidence from some South American or other excesses.

At The Public Good: Lessons for the 3rd Millennium, a conference organized to honour Hon. Allan J. MacEachen, a long-serving Liberal cabinet minister, on his home territory at St. Francis Xavier University in Antigonish, Nova Scotia, I became discouraged and totally dismayed after listening to Canada's "best and brightest" for several hours as they forecast that the high unemployment, then over 9%, and slow growth would continue well into the next century.[22]

When I couldn't take it any longer I took advantage of the opportunity provided by a floor microphone to suggest that we learn from the experience of the 1939-74 era and use government-created money to stimulate the economy and help finance the essential services being cut back due to budgetary restraint. The best that the then deputy-minister of finance, David Dodge, could say in reply was "Mr. Hellyer's solution would be inflationary."

I find it appalling that a man who has taught economics, influenced government policy during the years when Canada was reduced from a prosperous, progressive middle power to a mediocre one, and who was promoted to be the new governor of the Bank of Canada could reply so superficially. Any undergraduate student of economics would or at least should know that it is the quantity of money that is created that determines prices and not who creates it. The "M" in Irving Fisher's money equation, which is so popular with Friedmanites and neo-classical economists, means money – not   bank-created money or government-created money – just money.

One of America's genius inventors, Thomas Edison, put the whole question of bonds, bills and national credit in perspective.   "If the nation can issue a dollar bond it can issue a dollar bill. The element that makes the bond good makes the bill good. The difference between the bond and the bill is that the bond lets money brokers collect twice the amount of the bond and an additional 20 percent. [Total of principal and interest by the time the bond is paid off.] Whereas the currency, the honest sort provided by the constitution, pays nobody but those who contribute in some useful way. It is absurd to say our country can issue bonds but cannot issue currency. Both are promises to pay, but one fattens the usurers and the other helps the people. If the currency issued by the people were no good, then the bonds would be no good, either."[23]

That is true.   Duly elected legislatures are the custodians of the sovereignty once exercised by monarchs who held a monopoly on money-creation. Legislatures may delegate part of their power over money, but if they delegate all or most of it, sovereignty passes to the "money monarchs" who are fortunate enough to be the recipients of incredibly rich benevolence. Any country that doesn't control its own money supply is neither sovereign nor democratic.

CHAPTER 7

CAPITALIST TOTALITARIANISM

*"Contrary to its claims, capitalism is showing itself to be
the mortal enemy of democracy and the market."*

Dr. David Korten

One can understand why people like David Rockefeller and his colleagues would prefer a seemingly innocuous tag like New World Order to describe their plan for elite rule rather than give it a more precise definition which would be Capitalist Totalitarianism. That is the direction in which the world is headed despite all of the colourful rhetoric to the contrary. Democratic and human values are being replaced by corporate values and the notion that money is majesty.

The above quote from former Harvard professor David Korten tells the story better when it is put in context. "Contrary to its claims, capitalism is showing itself to be the mortal enemy of democracy and the market. Its relationship to democracy and the market economy is now much the same as the relationship of a cancer to the body whose life energy it expropriates.

"Cancer is a pathology that occurs when an otherwise healthy cell forgets that it is part of the body and begins to pursue its own unlimited growth without regard for the consequences to the whole. The growth of the cancerous cell deprives the healthy cells of nourishment and ultimately kills both the body and itself. Capitalism does much the same to the societies it infests."[1] It is not that business, subject to reasonable restraint by government, is bad. It has proven to be otherwise. But when it seeks to eliminate restraints imposed in the public interest, and pursues the unrestricted growth designed to eliminate genuine competition in the marketplace, capitalism crosses the line from benevolent to malevolent. The cancer is rampant.

The New World Order permits the repetition on a world scale of what happened in the United States in the late 19th century. A few families, including the Rockefellers, Mellons, Carnegies and Morgans, bought up everything in sight in order to eliminate competition and raise prices to achieve higher profits. These were ruthless people whose progeny have tried to rehabilitate the family names through their philanthropy. But their philosophy was personified by John D. Rockefeller, Sr. who bought out his competitors in the oil business because he didn't like "vicious competition."

For a while, in the 20th century, anti-trust laws stopped and reversed this trend and a number of giants were broken up. If that had not been the case there would have been no independent Bell Canada, for example. And if there had been no Bell Canada there would have been no Nortel. Anti-trust was good for small countries. But today anti-trust is in deep hibernation and there have been few recent cases that are worthy of note. The important news is that an attempt is now underway to extend market power across the globe because big companies are no more sanguine about competition from foreigners than they are from fellow countrymen.

That is the reason I smiled in the summer of 1997 when Federal Reserve Board Chairman Alan Greenspan told a luncheon meeting of the Washington Press Club[2] that what they were seeing was the ascendancy of market economics. What he should have told them is that what they were seeing was the ascendancy of market power economics, but on a global as opposed to a national scale.

A BIT OF CORPORATE HISTORY

The history of corporations is similar to the proverb of the camel being allowed to put its head inside the tent for warmth and, never being satisfied, pushes its way in and takes over the tent.

Corporations began as vehicles for the production of goods and services on a scale beyond the capacity of a single individual. They owed their existence to the sovereign people from whom they derived their power. Consequently, their objectives were limited; they could only do certain things. Often their charters were limited and only allowed to run for so many years, after which they had to account for their actions in order to have their charters renewed. The directors were liable for misdemeanours. Corporations had stakeholders other than shareholders.

In time, this accountability became irksome so corporations used their power and influence to remove the restraints, one by one. Their objectives were broadened so that they could invest in anything and do just about anything. Their charters were granted in perpetuity so they would outlive the people they were designed to serve. And the directors' liability was limited to a very narrow range so they could pursue policies that might have put them in serious jeopardy otherwise.

Most important of all, the United States Supreme Court granted corporations the status of persons. This gave them a profound advantage. As persons they were qualified to take advantage of the Takings Law which provides compensation to any person when government takes away their implied right to use their property for any purpose or in any manner they wish. This is a concept of law which was foreign to Canadian experience and which the U.S. rammed down our throats in NAFTA. Allegedly, Canada was a party to this bit of nonsense designed to keep the Mexicans in their place – but at what price? It was the basis for Chapter 11, of NAFTA, under which we can be taken to the cleaners.

Our government, not realizing what it had done, tried unsuccessfully to get the U.S. and Mexico to alter the

Chapter. Then Trade Minister Pierre Pettigrew said we would not sign another treaty containing such a clause.[3] Just a few weeks later, however, at Québec City, Mr. Chrétien emerged from his meeting with U.S. President George W. Bush and Mexican President Vincente Fox, both staunch supporters of the investor-protection measures, saying that Chapter 11 has not been a problem. "I think the clause has worked reasonably well in NAFTA, between Canada, Mexico and the United States," Mr. Chrétien said. "I do think it has worked very well."[4] He said investors have to have this protection in order to invest. This is such blatant rubbish that it boggles the mind. Canada was already one of the most foreign-owned countries in the world before NAFTA, and both the Ethyl Corporation and United Parcel Services, which have sued us, were doing business here long before they had the right to sue under Chapter 11.

The principle is wrong. Foreign corporations have greater rights in Canada than Canadian corporations, and that is wrong. Under NAFTA's Chapter 11 transnational corporations have equivalent status to nation states, and that is wrong. And not content with having this practice apply to Canada, the U.S. and Mexico, the transnationals obviously want it to apply to all the countries of the Americas, and then the world. They want to be able to tell every municipal, state or provincial and national government in the world that if they pass or amend any law that affect their profits, future profits or implied profits they have the right to sue for damages. One would be hard-pressed to find any quid pro quo for taxpayers who have to pick up the tab.

THE BIG FISH

Big corporations are like big fish. First, they swallow the smaller fish in their own pond and when there are no more they look for other waters to swim in. Their appetite is insatiable. So they get their political flunkies to negotiate treaties that give them the right to buy up, or otherwise eliminate, the competition wherever it may be found.

This includes the elimination of competition from

governments which spend billions of dollars on health care, education and other services. Such sums are viewed with covetous eyes by corporations. If they can persuade governments to abdicate direct responsibility in these areas there is money to be made – especially if governments continue to provide most of the funds. Everything is to be commodified, and a price attached. Old fashioned notions like "free and equal access" and the "common good" will be put on the same list as endangered species.

Financial markets manage the fish pond. In an era when there were plenty of small and medium size fish still to be swallowed up, the really big fish were able to sustain growth rates of 15% or more. Once it has been achieved for a few years, it becomes a benchmark of investors' expectations. But the rate is not sustainable. If the world economy is growing at an annual real rate of 2.5%[5] – perhaps about 5% in nominal terms – how many corporations can expect to continue to grow at 15% indefinitely? Not very many! If the average working person gets an annual real increase of 2%, or less, why should the monopoly players expect three or four times as much?

The thrust of globalized investment is to establish a new monarchy where the transnational corporations enjoy the trappings of royalty, including near-absolute power over the chattel workers they employ. Still they cannot aspire to nobler rank than that of Prince or Princess because they must bow the knee to those who hold their fate in the balance, the people who provide the credit necessary for them to expand their empires. It is the banking cartel which aspires to absolute power, the power of life or death for impoverished billions of our fellow travellers on planet Earth.

THE ABSOLUTE MONARCHS

The trend in banking, as in other industries, is toward an ever greater concentration of power and corresponding elimination of competition. In an earlier book entitled *The Evil Empire: Globalization's Darker Side*, I had a chapter called "The Banks Play Monopoly." In it I recalled how Canadian banks had bought all the major brokerage houses in order to take over the lion's share of that business. Then they complained about unfair competition from the trust companies. So, one by one, they bought all the big ones. At the time that book was published, only one large independent trust company remained, Canada Trust. That has since been taken over by Toronto-Dominion Bank and, as you might expect, branches are being closed, service reduced and transaction fees increased.

When the major banks had bought up most of their serious competition in the financial services industry, their next step was to try to merge and reduce competition further. Four of the majors – Royal Bank and the Bank of Montreal, as well as CIBC and the Toronto-Dominion Bank – filed applications with the Minister of Finance, Paul Martin, who wasn't pleased with the way they went about it, and put them on hold. In retrospect, this appears to have been more a political manoeuvre than a matter of conviction on the part of the government and the minister of finance. New legislation was passed in the spring of 2001 and now mergers will be entertained, and it may not matter whether or not fewer banks would be in the public interest. It only matters that it would be in the banks' interest. Competition would be further reduced, and the public less well served. But who cares? Certainly not the government.

It promises competition from new sources. Foreign banks will be given additional powers. But they are not going to start competing heavily in the retail market where more, rather than less, competition is needed. One of the foreign banks principal areas of activity will be to compete with Canadian banks in the creation of money to help foreign corporations buy Canadian companies. This is one area in which our banks have been prolific. A foreign corporation with a good credit rating can buy a Canadian company without bringing any new capital into the country. The assistance of our banks can best be described as anti-Canadian.

Even mergers will not put Canadian banks in the major league of world finance. But new legislation raising the limit of shares that can be owned by any one person or corporation from 10% to 20%, will put all of our major banks in jeopardy of being first controlled and later bought by foreign interests. We have been told that foreigners already own just under 10% of the shares of the Royal Bank and Canadian Imperial Bank of Commerce and are just salivating for the limit to be raised. It is easy to understand their joyful anticipation when you realize that banks have licences to print money. There is no other business like it!

It is sheer folly to put Canadian banks up for grabs in the global marketplace. They cannot survive the concentration that is occurring worldwide. The world's leading ten investment banks almost doubled their share of fee-based and advisory business in global capital markets between 1990 and 1998, to garner 77% of the market. This concentration of market share in the hands of the top banks coincided with an explosion in the global capital markets during the 1990s from less than $1,500 billion to $4,000 billion in eight years. And don't forget that this incredible increase in "capital" resulted from money being created by the banks and became, in their hands, the equivalent of an appropriation of assets. In other words, they are putting the world deeper and deeper in hock.

That is how the system works. In reality, the banks have turned the world into one humongous pawn shop. You hock your stocks, bonds, house, business, rich mother-in-law or country and the banks will give you a loan based on the value of the collateral. If you pay off the loan, with interest, they will give you back your valuables. But don't forget that there is only enough legal tender in existence to pay off about 5% of the loans outstanding at any one time. And if the market value of your collateral goes down, which happens periodically with the current boom-bust system, they may call your loan or require additional collateral at the worst possible time when thousands of others are in the same boat and there are not enough life rafts to go around. So the banks wind up appropriating your assets. They are aided and abetted in this transfer of assets by the central banks which have become little more than handmaidens to the counterfeiters.

CENTRAL BANKS AS DICTATORS

One of the new global myths is that central banks must be independent of politics and politicians. This highly questionable notion has taken hold over the years, thanks to the constant propaganda of the globalizers, and has achieved the status of holy writ. Blind acceptance was demonstrated when the first act of newly elected U.K. Prime Minister Tony Blair was to abdicate the power of his government and turn over to the Bank of England exclusive authority to set interest rates. It was an appalling decision for a social democrat. What he was saying, without realizing it, was that bankers are competent to make the most important decisions facing the lives of citizens but politicians are not. What happened to the theory of responsible government? It died with the abdication of responsibility. Democracy is dead. Long live the monetary dictatorship?

I find the whole idea highly repugnant. I believe, as Winston Churchill said, that democracy is the worst kind of government ever devised, except for all others. But I believe that the "except for all others" should be underlined. Most of us are familiar with the fallout from fascist and communist regimes, but how many of us have taken the time and made the effort necessary to review the havoc wreaked by central banks? The Bank of Canada, backed by ideologues of the same stripe in the federal finance department, has almost destroyed Canada. Actions of the Federal Reserve Board in the United States have put the Third World and developing countries so deeply in debt that they live without hope of ever enjoying the good life. Why should organizations that have caused more destruction than a handful of atomic bombs be trusted with dictatorial powers?

THE BANK OF CANADA

In 1974, when Gerald Bouey was Governor, the Bank of Canada (BOC) changed course and adopted monetarism, Milton Friedman's theory that the money supply should be increased by a pre-determined fixed amount each year, as official policy. That was the worst decision in the history of the BOC and whether it was Bouey's idea, or whether it originated with the Bank for International Settlements, we may never know.

The governors of the industrialized world's central banks and the chairman of the U.S. Federal Reserve Board meet regularly, in secret, at the headquarters of the BIS in Basel, Switzerland. This has all the trappings of a conclave of bishops and is so secret that not even ministers of finance are allowed to attend. It is alleged that the adoption of monetarism was a collegial decision. Whether true or not, the policy switch of central banks occurred more or less simultaneously.

Governor Bouey gave us a tentative trial run in 1974-75 when he induced a minor recession. It was a foretaste of things to come. Government revenues did not increase as fast as previously projected. Consequently, the deficit almost tripled from a little more than $2 billion to a little over $6 billion, and the net federal debt jumped from about $28 billion to just over $34 billion, by far the largest year-over-year increase since World War II.

It was, however, merely a warm-up for the main event scheduled for 1981-82. By then President Jimmy Carter's nominee, Paul Volcker, had become Chairman of the FED, in the United States. Volcker, who like his boss Jimmy Carter, was a distinguished member of the Trilateral Commission, was also a disciple of Friedmanism to the n'th degree. In 1979 he began tinkering with the U.S. money supply with weird and unpredicted results; but he decided to stay the course and put monetarism to the ultimate test.

The FED squeezed the system as it had never been deliberately squeezed before. Other central banks, including the BOC with Bouey at the helm, did likewise. Interest rates moved to historic highs as the growth of most economies came to a shuddering halt. Millions of innocent people lost their jobs. Hundreds of thousands of others lost their homes when they couldn't afford to pay the high interest rates. Tens of thousands more lost their farms, often after several generations in the family, and businesses went bankrupt on a scale unseen since the onslaught of the Great Depression – all victims of the most cold-hearted and inhumane economic manoeuvre in human history.

When you stop to think about it, can you think of anything more stupid than this? One branch of government, the Bank of Canada, deliberately and callously puts half-a-million people out of work. Then other branches of that same government start scrambling around trying to dream up new programs designed to put a few of those same people back to work. Can you think of any greater insanity? The result was more spending and a bigger deficit leading to more debt. Naturally, the politicians were blamed for responding to public pressure to repair some of the damage caused by the BOC's tight money, high interest rate policy.

The 1981-82 recession resulted in government revenues remaining flat – billions less than projected – while program spending had to be increased to pay for the "make-work" projects. The federal deficit took the biggest one-year jump ever from just over $15.5 billion to $29 billion and, thanks to high interest rates, the net federal debt followed suit rising from about $107.5 billion to $136.5 billion. The data for federal debt to GDP ratios in both the U.S. and Canada make it painfully clear that the subsequent debt crisis in both countries had their origin in the recession of 1981-82.

We had not yet recovered from the disastrous consequences of that recession when Bouey's successor as governor of the BOC, John Crow, gave it to us on the other cheek starting in 1988. A monetarist ideologue, he even beat the U.S. with his timing of the nasty punch. Our recession and the subsequent period of slow growth began before theirs and lasted longer – so long, in fact, that Professor Pierre Fortin, of the Université de Québec à Montreàl, labelled it the "Great Canadian Slump."

Crow overshot the mark in his zeal to achieve zero inflation. Not even the U.S. went that far and the different targets have been credited with the different unemployment rates in the two countries – the U.S. being little more than half those suffered in Canada. This had a profound influence on the difference in productivity rates between the two

countries.   High unemployment results in low productivity,
whereas low unemployment results in high productivity.   So
the productivity gap that occurred in the 1990s was primarily
due to bad management on the part of the Bank of Canada.
The   following   chart   shows   the   relationship   between
unemployment and output per member of the labour force.
As you can see, when unemployment is high, increases in
output are low, and when unemployment drops, output
increases.

Chart No. 4
Relationship between unemployment
and productivity

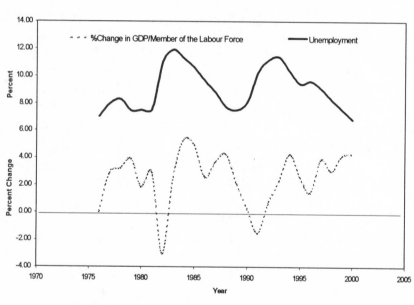

Source: Statistics Canada

In summary, the results of Crow's excess have been
disastrous.   In the aftermath of the 1990 and subsequent
squeeze, federal government revenues actually fell from $122
billion in '91-'92 to about $116 billion in '93-'94.   Tax rates
which were already too high, had to be increased to
compensate.   The federal deficit, which had dropped from
$38.4 billion in '89-'90 took off again to reach a high of $42

billion in '93-'94. Needless to say the debt continued to sky-rocket!

Gross incompetence is far too mild a description for Bank of Canada policies. They were nation wreckers! John Crow's mismanagement set the stage for the 1995 federal budget which was the worst in my memory and probably the worst in Canadian history. The cut-and-slash approach reduced a proud and progressive middle power to a very mediocre one. Many people have abandoned hope. This most disastrous of all budgets was allegedly the brainchild of the deputy finance minister, David Dodge, the current governor of the BOC, who persuaded finance minister Paul Martin, against his political instincts, that Draconian measures were required.

Apparently, other more sensible alternatives were not considered by Dodge and the handful of officials in the finance department, and the BOC, who were primarily responsible for running Canada into the ground. The alternative, even at that late stage of their continual bungling, was to use the BOC creatively to get out of the hole that they had dug just as had been done to escape the Great Depression.

In 1997 The Canadian Action Party retained the highly reputable Ottawa-based Informetrica Ltd. to do some computer simulations of what might be possible by means of a judicious injection of government-created money. The tests showed that it would have been possible to reduce unemployment from 9%, which it was then, to 4%, to balance the budget and to eliminate the hated Goods and Services Tax (GST), without replacing it with another tax, all within four years. Yet this option of using the people's own bank in such a positive and liberating way was not on the table. In my mind this raises serious questions about David Dodge's qualifications to be governor of the BOC.

At the time Dodge was appointed governor, Madelaine Drohan's column in the *Globe and Mail* was titled, "Central bank safe in Dodge's hands."[6] An editorial in the *Globe* provided similar assurance.[7] The BOC might be safe, but for whom? Safe in the sense of being good for the private banks, maybe. Safe in the sense of preserving the value of capital at the expense of other economic stakeholders, no doubt. But good for the shareholders? No way. The shareholders are the last on the BOC's list of concerns. The owners don't count!

The bottom line is this. The Bank of Canada bears a greater share of responsibility for the near-ruination of a beautiful country than do the politicians – even though the latter are guilty of being lap-dogs for an impossible system. So why should we abdicate democracy and put our destiny in the hands of financial dictators who have made such a botch of our affairs?

WHAT THE BANK OF CANADA HAS DONE TO CANADA, THE U.S. FEDERAL RESERVE SYSTEM HAS DONE TO THE WORLD

As I mentioned earlier, it was during the reign of FED chairman Paul Volcker that the world financial system became unstuck. Volcker, like most economists, misread the origin of the inflation of the late 1960s and 1970s and concluded that it was a monetary phenomenon which had to be tackled by monetary means. In 1981-82 he induced the worst recession since the Great Depression with predictable results. Not only were the social consequences enormous the economic consequences were equally devastating.

Economies slowed, government deficits increased and these were rolled over into debt and compounded at high interest rates. In the United States, the total government, corporate and personal debt, which had been remarkably stable at about 140% of GDP, suddenly took off and headed toward 190% in less than two decades – the highest since just before the Great Depression. So, although it is true that monetarism helped put the inflation genie back in the bottle, it is equally true that in doing so it let the debt genie out of the bottle with a debt time bomb in its hands.

While debt levels in the United States should be of some concern, it is the Third World debt that threatens the world financial system. It is that system, or more precisely the banking aspect of it, that is the source of the debt. It has been the policy of central banks, however, that has converted a problem into a global nightmare. The figures for growth of long-term debt for all developing countries put the whole matter of compound interest in frightening perspective. The following figures are all in U.S. dollars, rounded to the nearest billion. In 1970 their long-term debt was $61 billion. By 1980 the figure had increased to $452 billion, much of it due to new loans resulting from a surplus of petro dollars. Then came the shock! As a result of the high interest rates flowing from the FED-induced great recession of '81-'82, the total leapt to $1,243 billion in 1991. Thanks to compound interest it just kept growing until it reached $1,957 billion in 1998.[8] The figures for total debt are even worse. They increased from $610 billion in 1980 to $2.46 trillion in 1998.[9] That, unfortunately, is not the end of the story. The only way these countries can pay the interest on the debt, which in some cases exceeds their total foreign exchange earnings, is by borrowing more money and going deeper into debt. One doesn't have to be a seer to forecast the ultimate explosion.

CHAPTER 8

WINNERS AND LOSERS

*"Men occasionally stumble over the truth,
but most of them pick themselves up and hurry off
as if nothing had happened."*

Winston Churchill

WINNERS

The Banking Cartel

There is absolutely no doubt who the biggest winner in a globalized capital system without significant borders will be. It will be the international banks which dominate global finance. They are in a class by themselves because there is no business as profitable as that of printing money. So to the extent that nation states give up their sovereign right to print part or all of the money they require to keep their economies growing and prosperous, the big banks are the beneficiaries. Whoever prints the money gets the profit. If it is printed by and for the people, the people benefit. If it is printed by the banks as debt to be loaned to governments, business and individuals, it is the banks that reap the bonanza.

I have talked to many bankers about their business and although they understand well the mechanics of their trade it is only rarely that you can find one who understands the philosophical and moral consequences of a system that was never designed by economists for the betterment of mankind, but which just grew like Topsy under the watchful eyes of people who understood how profitable it can be. One banker who really understood the significance, and who was willing to share it openly, was Sir Josiah Stamp, a director of the Bank of England. He said: "Banking was conceived in iniquity and was born in sin. The Bankers own the earth. Take it away from them, but leave them the power to create money, and with the flick of the pen they will create enough money to buy it back again. However, take that power away from them and all the great fortunes like mine will disappear, and they ought to disappear, for this would be a happier and better world to live in. But if you wish to remain the slaves of Bankers, and pay the cost of your own slavery, let them continue to create money."[1]

This is the truth. As we saw in the previous chapter, the Third World is now so deeply in debt that there is no hope of them escaping the slavery of usury and enjoying that "happier and better world" that Sir Josiah envisioned unless the banking system is changed fundamentally. Even those of us in the First World find our hopes dimmed as we are obliged to pay such a large proportion of our income as interest on our debt that there is insufficient left to meet the legitimate needs of health care, education and other high priorities.

Transnational Corporations

Next to the banks, the transnational corporations are the big winners in the global casino. They will pursue their goals of growth by eliminating the competition through purchase or amalgamation in the private sector, and by mining the huge potential markets in the public sector as these are opened up to privatization. They will have the financial backing of the big banks which, in many cases, own large blocks of shares and have representatives on their boards of directors.

Individual winners are the chief executives and other officers of the multinationals who reward themselves with pay, bonuses and stock options which, increasingly, can best be described as obscene. The major shareholders also rank high on the list of beneficiaries, as do some retirement and mutual funds. These are often cited as justification for the insatiable growth of the multinationals. After all, it is argued, anyone can buy shares in these companies. They can, if they have the money. But the big gains go primarily to those who are already rich. In the U.S., for example, the wealthiest 1% of the population own 80% of the common shares, while the poorest 80% of the population only own 10 percent. So it requires a long stretch of the imagination to say that everyone benefits.

The Airlines

To some small extent the world's airlines prosper as a result of globalized investment. Officers and representatives of transnational companies have to circle the globe looking for opportunities and following up on the most promising ones. Their business, usually first class or business class, is eagerly sought by competing commercial carriers who are among the first to notice the effects of a global slowdown such as the one that occurred in the early months of 2001.

Some Workers in Developing Countries

There is little doubt that jobs transferred from the developed countries to the less developed and developing countries bring smiles to the faces of the recipients – at least for a while. Even though most of them work under the most appalling regime of low wages, unsatisfactory sanitary and environmental conditions, few if any benefits, and often subject to physical and/or sexual harassment, the majority view of both the workers and their politicians is that any job is better than no job. They do not enjoy the luxury of being able to escape the deprivations associated with the Dickensian era.

There is an alternative means of providing equivalent jobs which will be discussed in a later chapter. Without such an alternative, developing countries would be reluctant to give up the few crumbs that are being thrown their way.

Personal

Since globalization, my underwear falls off, my pyjamas don't fit, the roses I buy for my wife's birthday anniversary don't have the scent of roses and my latest pair of Clarks Wallabees, the first to be manufactured in the Far East, were the poorest quality and the most expensive of this brand of shoe that I have bought in the twenty-five or more years I have been wearing them.

LOSERS

All Democrats!

In my opinion the greatest casualty of globalized investment is democracy. Individuals all around the world, and the politicians they elect to represent them, are fast losing control over their own destiny. Although there are people who will argue that food is more important than freedom, history has shown that the human spirit prizes liberty above all else. And in the particular brand of slavery imposed by unfettered capital, the majority of citizens lose both their freedom to act and their ability to feed themselves, so they are being placed in double jeopardy.

There are people who argue that the solution is a world government with sovereign power to act on behalf of the poor and disadvantaged citizens of the world. They will admit, however, that the idea is a non-starter for the indefinite future because neither the United States nor China would agree to such a proposal, even if some countries might. In addition there is no evidence to suggest that it is a good idea.

There are some things that require international agreement and cooperation such as the protection of the oceans, and the species that live in the oceans, for example. Also the protection of the ozone layer and the fight against global warming, because no country can achieve the desired results on its own. The list is growing and includes biological weapons, weapons in space, new organisms, nanotechnology (self-replicating) and other developments of universal concern. Cooperation is essential, although the system breaks down when the world's one superpower opts out, as the U.S. has with the Kyoto Protocol and biological warfare.

While there is little doubt that the international approach is best for these life and death matters affecting the future of the globe, there is no evidence that centralized decision-making in the economic sphere is the best solution. That was the problem with the Soviet system. There were too many decisions being made by bureaucrats and party functionaries unfamiliar with the problems and unqualified to cope. This problem exists, albeit to a smaller extent, even in countries that call themselves democracies.

In Canada, for example, the East and the West often complain about too much power being exercised at the centre. The problem is exacerbated when decisions are made without adequate consultation. If Ottawa had worked more closely with Atlantic Canada in preserving the east-coast fishery, some serious mistakes could have been avoided. Even within provinces there are allegations of both neglect and ill-informed decisions. People in Northern Ontario have always felt that Queen's Park was either oblivious or indifferent to their problems.

As bad as this is, the frustration can be multiplied by ten when the decision-making authority is moved to New York, Paris, or Geneva. The decision-makers there are often totally ignorant of the facts and options important to the cases under review. This limitation applies equally in politics and in business. I remember when, years ago, what was then Standard Brands, of New York, bought Ingersoll Cheese, an important small industry in the Ontario town of the same name. Ingersoll had its own brand of superior cheese which was highly prized. It operated, for a while, under the new ownership but was soon shut down completely.

By happenstance, the Standard Brands executive who made both the decision to acquire Ingersoll Cheese, and then to close it down, was a guest at a small tourist resort in Muskoka that my wife and I have operated for many years.

So I asked him about the transaction, and the reasons for it. The Ingersoll plant, though profitable, was too small for a big multinational to be bothered with. What they were really looking for was increased market share for their own brands and that was really the aim of the game. Goodbye diversity! Goodbye local decision-making! Goodbye local employment! Hello globalization!

All Politicians

With globalization, politicians at all levels, municipal, state or provincial and federal, lose most of their power to make important decisions. It is what author Linda McQuaig has called *The Cult of Impotence*. Go to your favourite politician with a problem and they tell you how sympathetic they really are but there is nothing they can do because their hands are tied by their obligations under international treaties. They are really, really sorry, but ... .

If they are really sorry, you have to wonder why almost every month they sign another agreement giving away even more of their authority to govern. They don't call it sovereignty, but that is what it really is – sovereignty. It is the essence of control over our own lives and affairs. To be fair to all those politicians who really fall into the category of "rubber stamps", they are only going along with what the top dogs have put on their plates. But when all is said and done they are equally culpable, because they are putting party loyalty, and perhaps their own political futures, ahead of the real interests of the people who pay their salaries. Anything less than blind loyalty to party can carry a terrible price as some of us know from experience. But in the end – it is a question of personal priorities.

All Environmentalists

Anyone who cares deeply about the future of their planet, and the legacy they are leaving for future generations should be deeply concerned about globalized investment. Freedom from onerous environmental standards is a principal driving force behind the push for investment treaties. Charles Caccia, a former federal Liberal Minister of the Environment, is on the record as saying, "NAFTA has been an environmental disaster."[2] Indeed it has, if you look at the extra pollution from thousands of trucks carrying goods back and forth between the U.S., Canada and Mexico, the thousands of tons of American toxic waste being dumped in Ontario, and the risk this poses to drinking water, and the Toronto garbage that is being dumped in Michigan. And now the goal is to extend a NAFTA-type agreement to all the countries of the Americas – and then the world.

The attitude underlying the putsch was well stated by Abraham Katz, president of the U.S. Council for International Business, in a letter to Jeffrey Lang, Deputy U.S. Trade Representative, in March 1997, when he said: "We will oppose any and all measures to create or even imply binding obligations for governments or business related to the environment or labor." That is the attitude of big business. The reason they don't like democracy is because governments impose rules beneficial to citizens and environmental concerns. Big business wants to be its own referee when it comes to setting the rules and playing one government off against another. It is difficult to think of any greater recipe for disaster than to let such a force loose in the world.

All Small and Middle-Size-Countries

This item really includes the countries and the people who live in those countries. It means all of the world except for the five, or possibly six, major powers – the United States, Japan, Germany, the United Kingdom, France, and to a lesser extent, Italy. China, of course, will play its own pragmatic game. But for almost everyone else, globalization means the end of hope for industrialization, and any major drive toward self-sufficiency and self-respect. Bluntly put, it means colonial status! And in Canada's case, as I have already pointed out, first colonization and then, due to our unique geographical position next door to the elephant, annexation.

For all small countries, as well as middle powers, it is the iniquitous "national treatment" clause that is the vehicle for conquest. It is just as effective as marines and gunboats, and far, far more subtle because the local politicians tell the people that what is happening is in their own best interests, and that they should not protest or attempt to resist. And if they do, the police and armed forces of the country being colonized are mobilized against the protestors. How about that for a double fifth column?

Once the foreign powers have landed on your shore you don't really have a chance. If you develop an industry that shows promise and begins to capture a small but increasing share of the market for its product, the foreigners have the right to buy it, make it part of their empire, close it down or move it to another country. And if they decide to move it to another country there is no point in the workers attempting to buy the plant and machinery to produce the product because the same treaty prevents you from imposing a tariff on the product, and it is impossible to compete with labour being paid a dollar an hour or less.

In respect of the major global industries, if your country isn't already in the business, the cost of getting established will be too great to start. The existing transnational companies will squeeze you out of business and your government will not be able to assist you in the early days because that would be considered a subsidy, and subsidies are not allowed. If you breach this rule, the WTO will allow foreign countries to punish you by imposing tariffs on your other exports.

Furthermore, if the U.S. is successful in getting intellectual property protected under the GATS, the royalties that transnationals would charge for the use of their technology would be high enough to prohibit the establishment of a new business in the same line. That is what the GATS is all about. It is basically designed to prevent effective competition with the world leaders in each area of endeavour. It is probably the most effective form of protectionism, which is the word now used in the pejorative against any small country attempting to give its fledgling and underdog industries a break.

The summation of all these new rules, either existing or now being negotiated under treaties such as the proposed FTAA, and the GATS as part of the Uruguay Round under the WTO, is that no power that is not already a major industrialized power will be allowed to become one. They will all be relegated to perpetual colonial status. And in case anyone should think that this is just a collateral by-product of the New World Order they would be mistaken. It is the precise reason for globalized investment rules. The five (or six) major powers, which all became great industrial powers by protecting their industries, want the rest of the world as the feeding grounds to satisfy the appetite for growth which drives their established industries.

Nearly All Workers

One can almost hear the ghost of Karl Marx crying out, "Workers of the world unite; you have nothing to lose but your decent wages and working conditions." That is what the other half of globalization is all about. The first half was to protect the market power of the transnationals. The second half is to break the monopolies of big labour. As I pointed out earlier, the whole purpose of NAFTA was to provide American business with an unlimited source of cheap labour. A principal purpose of the FTAA, is to extend the poachers "open season" to all of the Americas.

Globalization affects workers in industrialized countries in several ways. The most immediate is the loss of jobs when production is moved to another country. Canada has lost 398,837 jobs as a result of NAFTA,[3] and the United States lost 766,030. These displaced workers' new jobs are likely to be in the service industries where most of the new jobs have been created but where wages are lower. In the U.S., for example, 99% of net new jobs created since 1989 have been in the service industry where average compensation is only 77% of the average in manufacturing.[4]

This contributes to an increasing disparity in the distribution of income and reduced purchasing power in the hands of the labour force. The situation would be comparable for Canada.

Another factor common to the two countries is the increasing use of threats by employers. Employers' credible threats to relocate plants, to outsource portions of their operations, and to purchase intermediate goods and services directly from foreign producers, can have a substantial impact on workers' bargaining positions. A *Wall Street Journal* survey in 1992, at the time NAFTA was being negotiated, reported that about one-fourth of almost 500 American corporate executives polled admitted that they were "very likely" or "somewhat likely" to use NAFTA as a bargaining chip to hold wages down.[5] A more recent survey by Kate Bronfenbrenner indicated that the threat rate during organizing drives has increased to 68% in mobile industries such as manufacturing, communications and wholesale distribution. Meanwhile, in 18% of campaigns with threats, the employer directly threatened to move to another country, usually Mexico, if the union succeeded in winning the election.[6]

Bronfenbrenner described the impact of these threats in testimony to the U.S. Trade Deficit Review Commission. "Under the cover of NAFTA and other trade agreements, employers use the threat of plant closure and capital flight at the bargaining table, in organizing drives, and in wage negotiations with individual workers. What they say to workers, either directly or indirectly, is if you ask for too much or don't give concessions or try to organize, strike, or fight for good jobs with good benefits, we'll close, we'll move across the border just like other plants have done before."[7]

Workers who object to globalization are tagged as protectionist. That's what the editorial writers and columnists call them. And, for once, they are right. Workers want to protect their wages and working conditions. And why wouldn't they? Big business wants to protect its capital and profits and is quite willing to adopt extraordinary measures to do so. It insists on protection against arbitrary measures by governments, even when they are in the public interest. But at the same time it wants to eliminate protection for workers and have wages set by "market forces".

This blatant double standard   is the genesis of increasing opposition to globalization. The benefits are all one-sided. Business has been trying to make a virtue of the jobs created in poor countries. It doesn't mention the jobs lost in developed countries. Nor does it mention that the cards are stacked in its favour and against the governments and people of the host countries that it invades.

Business Holds the Ace of Spades

Under the disputes settlement clauses in international treaties, like Chapter 11 of NAFTA, which is the model for the others, business can sue for lost profits if governments, at any level, change the rules. But governments do not have a comparable right to sue for damages if business changes its plans in a way that has a negative impact on taxpayers at large. Three case histories illustrate how the deck is stacked in favour of the business predators.

Canada Wire & Cable

Canada Wire & Cable Company Limited, a Canadian-owned company, was established in 1913. It was Canada's largest manufacturer of wire and cable with manufacturing plants in Montréal, Québec; Toronto, Simcoe and Smith Falls, Ontario; Fort Garry, Manitoba; and Vancouver, British Columbia. At one time it had 4,000 employees at its Toronto plant and sold Canadian manufactured wire and cable all over the world.

In the early 1990s Canada Wire was purchased by Alcatel Alsthom, the French multi-national manufacturer of the same types of products. As soon as the acquisition was complete, Canada Wire's market area was limited to North America so that it would not compete with Alcatel in other world markets. As a result, Canada Wire became unprofitable and Alcatel shut down its manufacturing facilities entirely. The huge Toronto manufacturing plant fronting on Laird Drive has now been completely demolished and is likely the site for the next Wal-Mart store. And what of Canada Wire & Cable? It now exists under the name Alcatel Canada Wire, the sales arm only for Alcatel of France. Needless to say, it was the Canadian taxpayers who paid the cost of Employment Insurance and re-training for the displaced workers, and not Alcatel. This in addition to the taxes lost.[8]

Bauer

When giant Nike Inc. stick-handled its way into Canada's hockey equipment business in December, 1994, by buying Canstar Sports Inc., as Bauer was then called, it gained control of some of the best-known brands in the game including Bauer, Cooper, Lange, Daoust and Micron. Any concern about the possibility of manufacturing jobs being lost appeared to be set at rest at the time of the takeover when Nike chairman Philip Knight said: "We plan to have Canstar continue to operate as an autonomous organization without any change to its structure, operations, management or personnel."[9]

Realists will not be surprised that plenty has changed since Nike gained control. The company changed its name and consolidated all its products under a single brand, Bauer. In addition it launched a thorough examination of its manufacturing operations with a view to outsourcing. On the same day that negotiations were to begin on a new union contract at its plant in Cambridge, Ontario, in April 1997, management abruptly cancelled the meeting, according to a union official, and employees were then told that the plant would close. Apparently all Nike wanted was Bauer's technology. Once they had that, they were free to move production to a Third World country.

Wherever Nike goes, controversy isn't far behind. The Beaverton, Oregon-based company has faced a storm of negative publicity over poor wages and working conditions at its subcontracted factories in Asia. That same year, 1997, it was stung by a U.S. labour group's report that Vietnamese workers were forced to run laps for failing to wear regulation shoes. Twelve women fainted and were taken to hospital. Nike subsequently suspended the manager and she was later charged by Vietnamese authorities.[10]

Dominion Textiles

This company was formed in the early 1900s with the amalgamation of Dominion Cotton Company and Montréal Cotton Company. It grew steadily and its list of CEOs looks like a page from Canada's Who's Who. Many of its trade names, including Texmade and Wabasso, will be remembered by old-timers.

Dominion Textiles expanded until it became the fourth largest textile producer, and the largest denim producer, in the world with manufacturing plants in Canada, the United States, Italy, France, Asia, England, Ireland, Hong Kong, South Africa, Singapore and South America. Sales peaked about $2 billion in the mid-1980s.

In 1995, however, it was bought by Polymer U.S.A., which wanted access to patented technology. Since that time all of the Canadian plants have been sold or closed.[11]

Our government tells us that direct foreign investment is essential to our future welfare. Much of what we have been getting, however, we can well afford to do without!

CHAPTER 9

ECONOMICS 2001

"The experience of being disastrously wrong is salutary,
no economist should be denied it, and not many are. "

J.K. Galbraith

Just because someone teaches economics doesn't necessarily mean that they understand it. That should be clear from the fact that we have had 45 recessions and depressions in the last two hundred years. It should also be clear from the chapter on capitalist totalitarianism, where I showed that central bank governors, several of whom had taught economics, had mucked up the Canadian and world economies to the point where bad solutions are proposed to remedy the effects of bad economic theory. Regrettably, the lack of understanding applies as much, and sometimes even more, to Nobel laureates as it does to lesser stars in the economic firmament.

Economics, like religion, is taught by rote. An idea is born. It is then nurtured and propagated until it becomes the mainstream theory widely taught and near-universally accepted by all except the occasional renegade. Nowhere has this been more evident than in the widely held view that recessions are inherent to classical market economics. When I asked my economics professors, more than fifty years ago, if recessions and depressions were necessary, the answers were far from satisfactory. I was given a brief resume of economic history which indicated that they had existed since the industrial revolution and consequently, by extension, they were part of the system.

It was no big surprise, then, when I did an unofficial poll of fifteen honours students in economics, that I got the same answer. Every one of them either quoted or paraphrased the same paragraph from the same book. But what if the chap who wrote the book was wrong? What if recessions and depressions are simply monetary phenomena which could be easily fixed if economists spent a little time and concentrated thought about possible solutions? Is it possible that our economic system just evolved like a wild weed while no one ever bothered to consider what kind of plant was needed to provide the nourishment and beauty that one would like to enjoy?

These are the questions that got me involved in politics in the first place and that are sufficiently intriguing, and desperately important in their consequences, to bring me out of retirement and back into the arena of political and economic ideas. I have the advantage – sometimes I think it is the disadvantage – of having lived through a whole cycle of economic certainty. As a child of the Great Depression I witnessed first-hand the devastating consequences of classical economics. Then World War II came along and broke the cycle of despair. After the War everyone was determined to do everything humanly possible to avoid a repetition of the dirty thirties.

One could say that was the reason for the ascendancy of the ideas of John Maynard Keynes, who had shocked fellow economists by attacking one of their most strongly held shibboleths. They had swallowed the classroom abstractions of one Jean Baptiste Say, who argued, in effect, that the capitalist system was self-correcting. Mavericks, often engineers, were claiming that there were times when there wasn't enough money floating around to buy all of the goods and services available for sale. Say scorned the amateurs, and insisted that all production created its own demand. Consequently there could be no such thing as what the economists called "a periodic shortage of demand", or purchasing power, as we would call it.

If Say had been right, as orthodox economists insisted, there would not have been periods of high unemployment. Keynes sided with the amateurs and started an intellectual storm that lasted for more than a generation. His theory that governments should spend more money when business was slow, and unemployment high, was heresy, but couldn't be ignored when it came from the pen of a respected professional. At the time I entered political life there were only a handful of dedicated Keynesians in Ottawa. A generation later, almost everyone was a Keynesian including the most unlikely of converts, U.S. President Richard Nixon. In two decades the exception had become the rule.

The Keynesian prescription of demand management worked acceptably well in the 1950s and early 1960s. Growth rates were good and interest rates were low, approximately equal to growth rates, so even though the debt grew, the debt to GDP ratio remained pretty well constant. The bigger pie was fairly divided between capital, labour and government and everyone was reasonably content. Then, in the latter part of the 1960s, something started to go wrong. Prices started to rise faster than had been considered normal and this gave rise to questions about the role of government in economics.

Professor Milton Friedman and his colleagues at the University of Chicago began to develop some new theories of their own. Friedman's research showed him that in a hundred countries, for a hundred years, price increases had been determined by the money supply. Inflation was the result of too much money being printed in relation to the goods and services available. Consequently, all that had to be done was to limit the amount of new money printed each year to some figure based on an estimate of the capacity of the real economy to grow, and inflation would be wrung out of the system.

While the theory had some technical merit, it was, alas, overly simplistic. It was comparable to saying that for a hundred years, in a hundred countries, summer had followed winter. Technically true, but without providing any clue as to whether or not the summers were hot or cool, whether they were wet or dry, and whether the crops were good or bad. Friedman's theorem reminded me of my very first course in economics which was entitled "The Hypothetical Handicraft Economy." But we don't live in some make-belief, hypothetical economy conjured up in the classroom. We live in a real economy that is extremely complex, with thousands of variables, that cannot be compacted into exact mathematical formulae.

Friedman's most fundamental error was to assume that there is only one kind of inflation – classic inflation – described as too much money chasing too few goods. This could only be true in a pure market economy where all prices, including labour, obey the law of supply and demand. But we don't have, never have had, and never will have a pure market economy of that hypothetical sort. We have an economy where many prices, including some of the most important ones, are based on market power which is just another way of saying monopoly, or oligopolistic, power. When this dash of reality is factored into the economic equation, the foundation for the Chicago School's "monetarist revolution" crumbles.

Professor Friedman recognized that the market for labour, for example, has been altered by legislation and regulation. In his book *Free to Choose*, where he discusses how the labour market works, he says: "Here, too, interference by government, through minimum wages, for example, or trade unions, through restricted entry, may distort the information transmitted or may prevent individuals from freely acting on that information."[1]

Quite so! But having observed and objected to the rigidities in the labour market due to government intervention, he proceeds to ignore the connection between wages and prices by denying the existence of cost-push inflation. He pretends that the system is self-regulating and that equilibrium will be restored by some invisible hand. Yet, after two disastrous recessions directly attributable to his theory, the kind of free market he dreams of and writes about does not exist. Nor will it in his lifetime or mine. He continues to ignore the rigidities he deplores. For him labour is just another price freely determined in the market.

This blind spot has been noted by many critics. In *Capitalism's Inflation and Unemployment Crisis*, Sidney Weintraub says: "To interpret money wages as 'simply another price' is to mistake flies for elephants." A general wage rise "comprises about 55 percent of gross business costs, closer to 75 percent of net costs, and probably even more of variable costs."[2] In fact money wages constitute the major factor in the economic equation: they far out-shadow any other price.

In view of this, one should not underestimate the significance of Prof. Friedman's unsubstantiated claim that "wage increases in excess of increases in productivity are a result of inflation rather than the cause."[3] This proposition flies in the face of the data. The Economic Report of the President, 1995, shows that wages outstripped productivity in the United States every year from 1964 to 1994. Not only did wages move up faster than productivity, they outpaced prices in 18 of the 21 years prior to the time Milton and Rose Friedman first published *Free to Choose* in 1980 – the exceptions being 1970, 1974 and 1979.

WAGES, PRICES AND PRODUCTIVITY

Monopoly power is not an easy subject for a politician to talk about because if there is one thing big business, big government and big labour have in common it is their reluctance to be identified as contributors to a problem. Yet for me to ignore the subject would be intellectually dishonest. It would be morally wrong to insist that the economic policies of the last 25 years, and those presently being followed, are inefficient, unjust, unstable, unsustainable and generally unacceptable without an analysis of how and why this is so, and what a better alternative might be. This, then, is not an exercise in assigning blame! It is an examination for discovery of what was, what might have been, and what should be in the years to come.

For more than a quarter of a century I have argued that the principal cause of the inflation which began to be a problem in Western industrialized economies in the mid-

1960s, could be explained by wage increases being out-of-joint with productivity. There have been oil shocks and a few other price changes which have produced blips, but the inflation trend line has been determined by the gap between nominal wages and real output.

The President's Council of Economic Advisers was right on target in its 1981 report in saying: " ... since payments to labor are estimated to account for almost two-thirds of total production costs, prices over the long term tend to move in conjunction with labor unit costs."[4] Precisely! In the longer term, prices move up at a rate that approximates the increase in wages and fringe benefits minus the increase in real output per person.

The data support the proposition as closely as anything in economics. The rate of change in the price level will approximate the difference between the average rate of change in money wages, including fringe benefits, and the average rate of change in the production of goods and services. If one looks at the data for a group of 15 Organization For Economic Cooperation and Development (OECD) countries, the long-term results, in most cases are quite close. The over-all average of averages is within one-quarter of one percent over a 27-year period. A correlation that close is very convincing![5]

The root cause of what has been called wage-push inflation has been dubbed "wage leadership" by a number of economists including Aubrey Jones, a former Tory cabinet minister and later Wages and Prices Commissioner under a Labour government in the United Kingdom. The most powerful union, in the most strategically advantageous position, sets the yardstick by which all subsequent negotiations are measured.

A Study of the Role of Key Wage Bargains in the Irish System of Collective Bargaining by W.E.J. McCarthy, J.F. O'Brien and V.G. Dowd underlined the significance in that country. "One of the most important conclusions to emerge is that wage leadership could give rise to rapidly rising prices even if all other factors contributing to the latter process were totally neutralized. This is so because key wage claims, induced by disturbed relativities, can initiate a general upward movement in wage relativities. This vital point has never been explicitly brought out in the substantial body of statistical, economic and econometric work which has already been published concerning inflation in Ireland. The principal reason for this is that these disciplines cannot cope with the institutional dynamics which lie at the heart of the problem."[6]

That is the nut of it. The science of economics has no mathematical formula to quantify a phenomenon that is as much political and sociological as economic. A phenomenon, nevertheless, with incalculable economic consequences.

The advent of "Free Trade" has made it much more difficult for many trade unions to negotiate wage increases in some industries, and in some cases new contracts have been stand-still, or worse. Some workers in the meat-packing industry were forced to agree to cuts, although the benefit of those lower wages never showed up at the meat counters in the supermarkets. It has been clear from the outset that curbing union power has been one of industry's key objectives in NAFTA and subsequent agreements and negotiations like the FTAA. Little wonder that unions are fighting back in the hope of achieving a fairer balance of power.

But regardless of the outcome, the question of wage leadership cannot be ignored. The most recent example occurred in Toronto when Local 4400 of the Canadian Union of Public Employees, representing caretakers, secretaries, language instructors, and other support staff employed by the Toronto Board of Education, went on strike in March, 2001. At the top of the union's list of demands was a pay raise. A report in the *National Post* stated: "The union is looking to make similar salary gains to the 8% raise teachers were handed last month."[7]

That is the way the system works. The teachers were granted 8% over two years, an increase of 4% a year, and the support workers, who had only had a 1% increase since 1992, demanded the same consideration. The principle applies to doctors, nurses, policemen, firemen, construction workers and just about anyone else with a little bit of leverage. If there is a good settlement in one part of the country, that will set the relativity target for the others.

This is a matter of extreme sensitivity at the time this book is being written in the late spring and early summer of 2001.

HEALTH CARE

Health care workers in various parts of the country are making substantial demands for improved pay, benefits and working conditions. I am in total sympathy, because they have been restricted for far too long. The workloads have increased to the point where care-givers are over-worked, over-stressed and unable to provide the kind of attention that they would want to give to their patients. Canadians owe a tremendous debt of gratitude to those who have stuck it out, while far too many have just packed their bags and left. But whatever is done will have to be considered as a one-time, emergency solution to meet what is obviously a crisis in the health care disciplines. It cannot and must not be used as a standard for other settlements across the board.

The problem is that any settlement greater than about 2% is inflationary. That is about the long-term increase in real output per person per year – in the best of times. So if any one group gets more than 2%, it will be at the expense of others. Either prices will rise, or unemployment will increase, or both. That was the sequence of events which led to the dreadful changes in policy that have caused such incredible damage in the last couple of decades.

And now, unfortunately, it doesn't really matter if someone hasn't had a raise for five or eight years. In justice, it does. But in the arithmetic of inflation, it doesn't. It is this year's increase in labour unit costs which will result in higher prices next year, not what happened last year or the year before. So, obviously, if we want to avoid the kind of cycles that have plagued us in the past we are going to have to change the system and opt for one that will provide more stability and predictability.

AN INCOMES POLICY FOR THE BENEFIT OF ALL

As early as 1961, I first predicted that there would eventually be a problem due to the exercise of monopoly power on the part of big business and big labour. In an address to the annual meeting of the Young Liberals of Canada, I described it as "a small black cloud on the economic horizon."[8] No one paid any attention because, even though unemployment in Canada was creeping up, inflation was insignificant so the problem was not obvious, and in accordance with the way we govern ourselves, there was no point in worrying until a crisis arose.

Ten years later the problem was obvious, even if the solution wasn't. The inflation rate was climbing and this became a matter of general concern. It was at this point that I wrote my first book on the subject entitled *Agenda: A Plan for Action*.[9] In it, I not only traced the source of what had gone wrong, but went on to propose that a very simple incomes policy would effect a cure. Where monopoly power existed in the hands of big business and big labour, it would be subject to mandatory profit and wage guidelines.

Profit guidelines for businesses would be based on long-term averages of return on capital for that industry. Wage guidelines for union contracts would be based on the average increase in real output per person in the labour force for the previous year. Guidelines would only apply in cases of monopoly or market power. This would include salaries for members of parliament, judges, and other cases where wages are set arbitrarily. Where genuine markets exist wages and profits would be determined by the market.

Two years before I wrote *Agenda,* I discussed the theory of limiting monopoly power by means of an incomes policy with the then Prime Minister, Pierre E. Trudeau, over lunch at his residence at 24 Sussex Drive in Ottawa. He listened carefully and seemed to be impressed. When we came out, my Executive Assistant (Housing) Lloyd Axworthy was waiting for me in the foyer. Trudeau looked at Lloyd , shook his head, and said: "That boss of yours!" I took it to be meant as a compliment.

I discussed it with him again over lunch some years later when the Liberal Party was trying to persuade me to run in a by-election in Toronto. His office arranged for the two of us to meet at Sussex Drive. By the time the day came I told him that I had decided not to run, but said I would like to take advantage of the opportunity to discuss economics with him and he allowed me to review the entire proposal in detail. It took the better part of an hour. When I was finished he gave me the most intelligent cross-examination that anyone has ever done on this subject. Pierre often claimed that he didn't understand economics, and there were times when he gave that impression. But that wasn't my experience on that occasion. He asked a string of questions that lasted almost an hour at the end of which he said: "Well, you seem to have all the answers." His single remaining consideration appeared to be that the guidelines didn't apply to chief executive officers, and their often unseemly increases. That is really a separate problem which has become even worse in the intervening years to the point where the total of salary, bonuses and stock options, in many cases, can only be described as obscene. This is a matter that will have to be addressed by social pressure on the one hand, and shareholders' wrath on the other.

As the years went by, his government tried other options such as wage and price controls which, as I had explained to him, should not even be considered except in cases of wartime emergency. Then he applied the six and five rule designed to reduce settlements by one percent a year, which would have worked successfully if it had been pursued until settlements reached two percent, and inflation has been wrung out of the system. I often wondered why he had never introduced the guidelines we had discussed.

Years later, when the two of us were having lunch at a little restaurant in Montréal, the subject arose again. We were discussing economics and he obviously was one hundred percent on side concerning the mandatory guidelines to control monopoly power. So I put the question to him directly. Why hadn't he introduced the system when he was prime minister, and had the opportunity? He looked at me somewhat wistfully, and said: "Because people said I was a communist." I knew what he meant. He was afraid that something that would be construed as government interference, but which I have always argued is perfectly justified under the best liberal principles, would reinforce the notion that his philosophy was rooted in the far left. It is a pity that he felt constrained in that way.

Had the system been installed in the early 1970s, we could have avoided the small recession of 1974. Furthermore, we might, just might, have turned our backs on the Friedman solution and avoided the two dreadful recessions to follow. But we didn't, and the situation continued to deteriorate as the chorus demanding action grew louder all the time, reaching a crescendo near the end of the decade in advance of the debacle of 1981-82. It was at this stage that I wrote a second small book entitled *Exit Inflation*, published in 1981.[10]

The situation had worsened sufficiently in the intervening decade that a new element had to be added. That addition was a 12 month wage and price freeze to reduce the inflation rate to zero, or very close to it. Neither wages nor prices would have increased for 12 months which would have provided the system with a clean slate from which to start anew. At the end of the freeze, the new mandatory guidelines would have been put into place to prevent the whole cycle from starting all over again.

There is no need, and insufficient space, to repeat here all of the fine print such as the exemption of internationally traded commodities, and farm products at the farm gate, provisions for wage catch-up in the guidelines, the method of averaging profits and other important details. All that is needed at this point is mention of the broad principles involved and the philosophical and economic rationale for such a policy.

The idea of limiting monopoly power is widely held in liberal circles. It goes back at least as far as the Sherman Anti-Trust Act in the United States, which was enacted near the end of the 19th century. Variations on the theme have been applied intermittently ever since. While the need to control monopoly power seems painfully self-evident, there is a political maxim that states the case most clearly. The English philosopher and political scientist, John Stuart Mill, put it this way: "The freedom of any person or group ends at the point where it trespasses on the freedom of another person or group." I have never found any better test in politics or law. In the case in point, big business and big labour were exercising their market and monopoly power in a way that was detrimental to the public interest and, consequently, limits to the exercise of that power had to be applied for the common good. Before anyone tunes out on the basis of self-interest, I would urge them to consider the consequences of our inaction which are almost beyond belief.

WHAT MIGHT HAVE BEEN

I tried to have econometric simulations done of what the Canadian economy would look like today if an incomes policy had been applied before the 1974 recession, which resulted in the first significant jump in federal debt. Unfortunately, there were too many variables, and there is no software designed to cope. So I have been restricted to some ballpark estimates which are not scientific, but which will provide a good idea of the order of magnitude of what might have been.

- If an incomes policy had been applied prior to 1974 there would have been no need for the recession of that year, the great recession of 1981-82, or the devastating follow-up one in 1990-91 leading to the great Canadian slump of the 1990s.
- Federal and provincial net debts would have remained at approximately their 1974 levels.
- Even if action had not been taken until 1981, net federal and provincial debt would have remained at approximately the 1980 level of $111 billion.
- In that event Canadian taxpayers would have saved approximately $643 billion in interest payments since that date – an amount greater than the net federal debt.[11] Just

imagine what could have been done with that much money.

- We would have avoided the social upheaval of people losing their jobs, houses, farms and businesses as a result of the recessions.
- Our gross domestic product would have been much higher. Informetrica, the Ottawa-based economic fore-casting company, estimates that we were under-producing by about $65 billion a year during the 1990s, due to excessive unemployment. Had we been operating at capacity the extra tax revenue would have provided even greater opportunities for tax reductions and better public services.
- Canadian productivity would have been much higher due to higher employment levels, and this would have closed much of the gap in standard of living between us and the U.S.
- There would have been no Rae days (compulsory time off without pay imposed by Ontario Premier Bob Rae).

In summation, the Canada of today could have been proud and prosperous. We could easily have afforded all the things that were cut back by governments which never needed to go into deficit financing in the first place. We could have undertaken vast new initiatives, and still had money enough left over to keep tax rates competitive with our neighbours, or better. One act of omission spelled the difference between merit and mediocrity.

WHAT IS

Instead of paddling our own canoe we decided to adopt the new American version of classical economics, being propagated by Milton Friedman in consort with the Trilateral Commission and associated groups, under the name of monetarism. The Bank of Canada, along with the central banks of other Western industrialized countries, accepted the doctrines of the monetarist counter-revolution in 1974, and endorsed it as their own. We weren't told very much about it, except that it was the only idea around for fighting inflation. It achieved some success in that direction, but only in part, and with negative consequences that are inestimable.

Of course it is not the only way to fight inflation. For cost-push inflation, as I have already explained, an incomes policy is infinitely superior to high interest rates. There are also alternatives in other situations. If real estate prices are rising too fast in Toronto, down payments can be increased until the market cools. If the stock market is inflating, margin requirements can be increased. And if consumer prices are rising, bigger minimum monthly payments on credit cards would dampen shoppers' enthusiasm. These measures can be adopted locally or regionally. There is no need to carpet-bomb the whole economy.

Apart from the two horrendous recessions, the effects of monetarist, or neo-classical, economics have included higher unemployment, higher debt, higher interest rates, increased volatility and lower production. It is a most unimpressive record, and yet we are constantly being brainwashed to believe that it is the economics of hope for a globalized New World Order. If the propagandists were honest enough to produce the data from 1974 on, most of us would choose the Old World Order in preference to the New.

If you compare the data for the years 1949-1973 with the period 1974-1998 – the 25 years after Friedmanism was adopted by the central banks – you will see the dismal results. In Canada the average increase in GDP dropped 43% from 4.9 to 2.8 percent. Unemployment increased by 90%, from an average of 4.74% to almost 9 percent. All of this resulted in a monumental 2,289% increase in federal debt.[12]

The increase was not primarily due to overspending on government programs, as the right insists. It was primarily due to the slow growth of the economy and debt compounding at high interest rates due to neo-classical policies. Compound interest was the real culprit as Chart 5 illustrates so dramatically.

The data for Australia are comparable. The rate of increase in GDP fell 38% in the second period and unemployment, which had been less that 2% prior to 1973,

increased to more than 8 percent.[13] U.S. data are not too
different. Increase in output was down 38%, unemployment
was up 41.7% and the average inflation rate was 102%
higher.[14] Finally the U.S. federal debt which went from
$266 billion in 1948, to $466 billion in 1973, reached $5.4
trillion in 1997, an increase of 1,052% in the 24 years after
monetarist, neo-classical economics came into effect.[15]

It is the world data which are most thoroughly
depressing. For the years 1950-1973 the average annual
compound growth rate of per capita GDP was 2.90 percent.
From 1973 to 1995 it was down to a disastrous 1.1% – more
than a 50% reduction.[16] So when you see pictures of under-
nourished children, or read about the millions who cannot
afford to go to school, or even the homeless people in
Montréal and Toronto, there is a reason for it. That reason is
bad economic theory resulting in bad economic management.

Chart No. 5

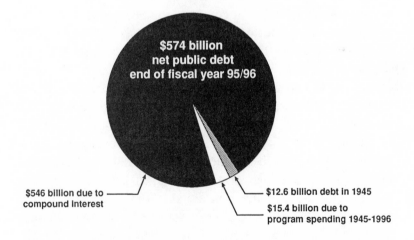

Sources: Public Accounts of Canada, 1995-96 and Department of Finance

So the next time you pick up your morning newspaper
and read a column or editorial which refers to "the
unquestioned benefits of globalization," and there are literally
dozens that do, think of the data. Write a letter to the editor
asking for the data behind the unequivocal assertion.

The empirical evidence is right before their eyes. Take a ten-minute walk through downtown Toronto and count the number of panhandlers. Talk to someone familiar with the facts about the thousands of people who are homeless, many of them sleeping on the streets. Or volunteer to help at one of the food banks. In 1974 there was not one food bank in Canada – not one! The first was opened in 1981; today there are at least 615 food banks with an additional 2,213 agencies helping hungry people across the country.

You would think that economists who can turn a blind eye on all of this misery would at least be influenced by the numbers, which are their stock in trade. But once you get "that old-time neo-classical economic religion", facts must not be allowed to interfere with faith.

I thought of this when I read an article by economist and regular *National Post* columnist, William Watson. I had the pleasure of meeting Professor Watson when we both appeared on a globalization debate aired by TVO Ontario. I found him to be a most amiable chap who also happens to be a "true believer" when it comes to the benefits of globalized *laissez-faire* economics. His article, which was designed to prove that globalization had been good for the poor of the world, was based on data for the last 50 years. In other words he had to include those 25 Keynesian years, which most "true believers" speak of with disdain, in order to raise the 50-year average enough to prove his point.[17] If he had just included the 25 years when his ideas have been in effect, he would have proved that the promise held out for globalized neo-classical economics is a fraud. It is interesting to note that the president of the World Bank, too, uses the 50-year data because the relevant 25-year statistics would not support the thesis that acceptable progress is being made in the war against poverty.

MICRO EFFICIENCY – MACRO MADNESS

It is clear from both the sights and sounds of poverty and despair, and the economic data which explains it, that we have gone from a system that worked reasonably well in the post-World War II era, to one that has a record of failure. Not only has neo-classical economics been less productive, it has contributed directly to an increased income disparity between the poor and the rich and between poor countries and rich countries. Promoters of globalization admit sheepishly that this is true, and consequently one of the problems that must be addressed. But if you listen carefully to their speeches, they never reach the point where they explain how this is to be done. Nor can they, because the system they are pushing is designed to increase rather than diminish income disparity.

The problem is that neo-classical economics concentrates almost exclusively on micro efficiency. If two companies merge, or one is taken over by another, the work-force is usually downsized. If the same amount of work is performed by fewer people that is more efficient. In many cases the survivors are over-worked and soon stressed out, but that relates to the quality of life which can't be found in the neo-classical equation. What happens to the fired workers, however, is critical to the overall economic numbers even if it is irrelevant to each individual transaction.

In classical theory they are supposed to find equally good or better jobs, so they will be as well or better off and the economy as a whole will benefit from the whole process. In practice, however, they may wind up taking lower paid jobs because they are the only ones available, or they may opt for early retirement, in which case the macro numbers are diminished.

The same problem can arise when production is moved to a Third World country. The result is often fewer jobs and lower wages. This means that a lot of people have less money to spend which creates a drag on the economy as a whole. The whole question of a shortage of purchasing power rears its ugly head one more time.

The same question arises when governments collect more money in taxes than they spend back into the economy. Paying down debt is admirable in theory, and every prudent person and business should do it. But when governments pay down their debt, and cancel bonds, they reduce the money supply and this has a dampening effect on the economy. As Milton Friedman concluded in his *A Monetary History of the United States*, it was a 30% plus contraction in the U.S. money supply in the years immediately following the stock market crash which was responsible for the Great Depression. A massive injection of money was required to get the economy rolling again and that didn't really happen until the outbreak of World War II.

The periodic or chronic shortage of purchasing power is intrinsic to the system, and it is not going to go away. To the extent that owners of capital make an after-tax profit and do not spend all of it back into circulation a shortfall in demand for the goods and services they produce will occur. This will result in unemployment unless new money is created at a rate which makes up that shortfall and allows the economy to continue to grow.

THE JAPANESE ECONOMY

The Japanese economy is a perfect example of a fine machine that is just idling due to the constrictions imposed by the neo-classical model. In true classical style, the Japanese banking system created too much credit money which allowed nominal prices of real estate and common stocks to escalate unreasonably. Then, as always happens, someone stuck a pin in the credit balloon and the whole system began to deflate. The value of real estate held as bank collateral declined sharply, as did that of the common shares held by the banks in their own accounts. The combination was a recipe for financial disaster. Inevitably, this affects the real economy which it certainly did in Japan. The economy slowed markedly and eventually came to a grinding halt.

Japan's Ministry of Land, Infrastructure and Transport said that property prices fell 4.9% in 2000, lengthening the country's real estate slump to a decade. The construction and development companies, which were among the banks' biggest customers, have been badly hit. The trend toward lower prices may be easing somewhat, but Sanyu Appraisal Corp., Japan's largest real estate firm, expects real estate prices to drop an additional 50% during the next few years.[18]

Monetary and fiscal policy, the two high cards of economic policy, have both been tried, but without success. The Bank of Japan has lowered effective interest rates to zero percent. But there is an old axiom which applies. You can lead a horse to water, but you can't make it drink. If people are uncertain about the future, and worried for fear that an economic recovery may be years down the road, they will not borrow, even at a low interest rate. On the fiscal front, the government has been borrowing money in an attempt to prime the pump – the Keynesian approach. But the water level has dropped too low for orthodox pump-priming to get the system flowing again.

The Joker of orthodoxy has also been played. Vast sums of public money have been used to bail out the banks. And the end is not in sight. The justification for this public largesse is that the consequences of major bank failures would be so great, and would have such a devastating effect on public confidence, that extraordinary measures are really in the public interest.

It is little wonder that Japanese voters became so disillusioned with politics and politicians. Nothing that had been tried worked. Cynicism prevailed. This set the stage for the triumphal entrance of the new Japanese Prime Minister, Junichiro Koizumi, with his unorthodox campaign promises of far-reaching structural reforms of his country's business and political practices. "My posture is not to fear pain, not to flinch from the barriers erected by vested interests and not to be shackled by past experiences, so as to establish an economic and social system that befits the 21st century," he said. "The top priority entrusted to me is to reinvigorate the economy and establish a society that's full of confidence and pride."[19]

Those are brave, wonderful words designed to inspire confidence. A little short-term pain is required in order to guarantee long-term gain. I am reminded of similar thoughts uttered by Canadian political leaders as they proceeded to dismantle the country. I strongly suspect that public confidence in Mr. Koizumi, too, will prove to be misplaced. Much of his program, and most of the advice he is receiving, is the same old classical nonsense that was being dished out in the 1930s and far too often since.

Mr. Koizumi recognized the malaise when he said: "Since the 1990s, the Japanese economy has struggled for a long time, people have lost faith in politics and there is an air of stagnation in society."[20] That is a correct analysis, but it is totally inconsistent with the prescription that follows. Mr. Koizumi seems determined to tighten not only the government's belt, but also that of its citizens. In his first policy speech after taking office he said he intended to cut "unnecessary government projects or transfer them to the private sector and reduce funding for government-linked special corporations."[21] These policies might make sense in a bustling economy but for the foreseeable future they spell additional stagnation.

Banking reform tops the list of policies that could wreak additional havoc. There are so many bad loans that many of the banks are technically insolvent and more could be after new rules come into effect at the end of September, 2001. They will force Japanese lenders to book gains or losses on their large portfolios of securities, rather than value them at purchase price as they do now.

The fear is that without major reforms the economy could remain in the doldrums for years without recovering. The proposed medicine, however, could make matters even worse, in the interim. There is a push to have banks unload bad debts and liquidate the collateral which they have been loath to do. Unfortunately, pulling the plug on thousands of businesses would further dampen the economy and put more people on the breadlines at a time when unemployment is already at a record high 4.9 percent.

What the Japanese economy needs, of course, is a massive infusion of debt-free, government-created money. Some of it should be used to buy the bad loans from the banks in order to give the struggling businesses the chance to survive rather than forcing them into bankruptcy which would only increase unemployment, and have a further dampening effect. Some of the new money could be used to cut taxes, and the balance for essential government expenditures. There are important infrastructure projects in need of attention and significant expenditures are required to undo some of the environmental damage that occurred when Japan's number one priority was rapid industrialization. The overall goal is to restore confidence, get the Japanese economy up and running again, and then keep it running without any increase in public debt. The Japanese have a heaven-sent opportunity to renounce the old ways and lead the world into a new millennium of positive and egalitarian economics.

It is painfully obvious from the Japanese situation, which is merely representative of dozens of situations that have occurred in dozens of countries from time to time in the last 200 years, that orthodox economics is woefully inadequate. It is really worse than that. It has caused so much human suffering and degradation that its effects can be honestly classified as a crime against humanity. True, we have made incalculable progress in many areas in the last two centuries. But much of this has been in spite of economic orthodoxy rather than because of it. When one considers the potential that has been lost, and what might have been accomplished, the shortfall is staggering. So it is long since time for the dismal science to take a look at its collective self in the mirror with the objectivity of an aging Dorian Gray. Hope springs eternal, and a re-incarnated discipline in economics is not beyond the realm of imagination.

P.S. If any of your economist friends speak harshly of this chapter, please ask them to send you a copy of their written report showing how to reduce world debt to sustainable levels and ensure the total debt to GDP ratios decline continuously for decades and centuries to come. Take a critical look at the report and send me a copy to double-check.

CHAPTER 10

A BETTER VISION

"There is a great day ahead. The future is on its side.
It's going now through the wilderness,
but the promised land is ahead."

Martin Luther King, Jr.

A very disturbing aspect of globalization is the fact that many of its most ardent supporters can't say what the world will look like when the process has run its course. Dr. Sylvia Ostry, one of Canada's chief negotiators in the Uruguay Round of trade negotiations which led to the WTO, has said: "We had no idea at the outset how much sovereignty would be given up, nor what the world would look like when we were finished." A similar view was expressed by Dr. Ronald Lehman, a senior U.S. negotiator under both Democratic and Republican administrations, who admits that the outcome is uncertain. Well, after giving the matter much thought, I can fill in the blanks for them. The results of unrestricted free trade and unrestricted global investment, for the majority of the world's inhabitants, can be summed up in one word – disaster.

It wouldn't be fair to say that the majority of economists and world leaders have got it all wrong without suggesting a better alternative. That point is often raised during the question period following my lectures in which I have been highly critical of the prevailing conventional wisdom. People ask: "What would you do?" Before answering, let me begin with a summary of the inevitable consequences of unrestricted free trade and foreign investment.

THE WAY WE ARE HEADING

- Most important of all, the majority of people worldwide will lose any effective control over their own destiny.
- The rich will get richer and the poor poorer, at least relatively.
- Unemployment levels worldwide will remain much higher than necessary.
- Periodic recessions and depressions will continue to occur.
- Every small country will lose control over its own destiny.
- It will be impossible for small and medium-size countries to achieve any significant degree of self-sufficiency.
- The rich countries will get richer in comparison to poorer countries.
- Canada, due to its unique geography, will be absorbed by the U.S.
- Civil wars will persist as a function of poverty.
- This kind of poverty will be exacerbated as small farmers and small plantation owners all over the world are squeezed out of business by the multinationals.
- People everywhere will become more dependent on a few transnational companies for their food supply.
- Infrastructures everywhere – except user pay – will continue to crumble.
- World debt will continue to rise – an effective curb on infrastructure renewal.
- Environmental concerns, and saving the planet for future generations, will take a back-seat to commerce.
- Federal, state or provincial, and municipal governments will become increasingly impotent to meet the legitimate demands of their people.

- Democracy – government of, by and for the people – will be effectively dead.

If you read the above list carefully, and thoughtfully, you will understand the reasons for the protests against the WTO at Seattle, the IMF and World Bank at Washington, the FTAA at the Summit of the Americas in Québec City, and against George W. Bush and leaders from the 15-nation European Union (EU) at Gothenburg, Sweden, and myriad other demonstrations that are becoming as frequent as summer storms. Different protesters may be driven by different concerns, but they have one thing in common – they don't like the way the world is being run, and they are not going to sit idly by and do nothing. The particular brand of capitalism being rammed down the world's throat by the Trilats and their affiliated hucksters is too good for them, and not good enough for the rank-and-file citizen of planet earth. So the protests will continue until the world leaders change course.

We, if I may include myself in this heterogeneous group, are unimpressed by those leaders who say that the protests are a threat to democracy. On the contrary, the protests are the only hope of ending corporate rule and saving democracy from a leadership which, perhaps unwittingly, is determined to end it. It is a leadership which will not listen to opposing views. To paraphrase the Bible, "They have ears to hear, but they will not hear." Or, to use a more modern vernacular, they pretend to listen but it is simply a case of in one ear and out the other.

A BETTER VISION

It is fair to assume from what I have said so far that I believe the Western world is totally void of inspired leadership. Certainly that is true of the G7, or G8, group of industrialized nations, for which there is ample evidence. Each one, in turn, has been seduced by the Trilats and their super-effective worldwide propagandists.

An inspired leadership might be concerned about the inexorable concentration of wealth and power and resolve to take steps to end or at least mitigate the trend. It would be concerned about the loss of sovereignty by people and nations and wonder if this was really in their best long-term interests. It would start from the premise that there is already enough wealth in the world to provide every one of its citizens with a minimum standard of food, clothing, shelter, education and health care in less than a decade, and take steps to transform their rhetoric of concern into the reality of a successful war against poverty.

To put flesh on these dry bones would mean winding up the IMF, liquidating the World Bank or reducing it to an aid agency, reducing the leverage of the banking system and using the occasion to pay off all Third World and developing country debt, abrogating or renegotiating all of the myriad bilateral or regional trade treaties, including NAFTA, in order to eliminate the "national treatment" clause, and winding up the WTO and subsequently replacing it with new Marquis of Queensberry trading rules that would guarantee "fair trade" for all countries rather than "free trade" which is tailor made for the benefit of the giants.

Listing all of these items in one paragraph may diminish the immediate impact, but what is being suggested is an intellectual and political revolution comparable to the industrial revolution or the knowledge revolution. We have become so caught up with the information age that we forget that knowledge can be used for good or evil, and that it can be quite useless if it isn't applied with wisdom. Getting everyone hooked up to the Internet is a wonderful idea, but it won't feed the hungry, clothe the naked, provide shelter for the homeless or make the sick well. These needs can only be met if the essentials for survival are given a priority comparable to the non-essentials which add lustre to life but don't provide for life itself.

GOODBYE IMF

As I pointed out in Chapter 4, the IMF lost its *raison d'être* years ago and neither of its two current functions are in the best interests of the global community. To use taxpayers money to rescue international financial institutions was not exactly what the signatories to the Bretton Woods agreement had in mind in 1944. The IMF's other contemporary role is to interfere in the internal affairs of nation states in a most unseemly manner.

Canadians may be surprised to learn that not long before the disastrous 1995 federal budget a letter from the IMF urged Finance Minister Paul Martin to cut health care and education transfers to the provinces, as well as UI benefits and funding for social housing. In his budget Martin announced spending cuts of more than $29 billion over the next three years in exactly those areas suggested by the IMF and in doing so, set Canada firmly on the road to mediocrity.

It is the Third World and developing countries that have paid the highest price for IMF involvement. Their hopes and dreams are routinely smashed. Joseph Stiglitz, former chief economist at the World Bank, describes how it operates. "In theory the fund supports democratic institutions in the nations it assists. In practice, it undermines democracy by imposing policies."[1]

An American commentator described the IMF and World Bank generously as balancing wheels. A better description is that they act as giant assault tanks, plowing through the fields and forests of underdeveloped countries, clearing a path for the invasion by foreign investment capital intent on exploiting the forests, mines, industries and financial institutions of what, for all practical purposes, is a captive nation bound by the chains of external debt. The IMF role of forcing its client countries to adopt Draconian economic policies is, in a word, abominable.

As I explained in an earlier book, it is only after spending a little time investigating what the IMF has been up to these last twenty years that one becomes hostile. I know from talking to friends on both sides of the Canada-U.S.

border that the majority are totally unaware. The exceptions are those who have actually worked in one of the affected countries, and witnessed first hand the devastation wrought in the name of "aid".

The institution cannot be redeemed, so it must be wound up and its assets used to help pay down Third World debt.

AU REVOIR, WORLD BANK

When I began to write an earlier book, *Stop: Think*, my inclination at the outset was to recommend that the World Bank be streamlined, reformed, made more transparent and more accountable – all of the clichés that I had read, or heard, emanating from world leaders and world bank officials who realized that the half-century old institution was under legitimate attack. As with the IMF, however, the more I learned about its operations and practices the more jaundiced I became. In the end I concluded that it had adopted the undemocratic policies of its sister financial institution, the IMF, and that there is no way it can be satisfactorily reformed.

I use "au revoir" rather than "goodbye" for the World Bank because, for it, there are really two options. It could be wound up, or it could be stripped of its lending function and become a relief agency with a pool of capital large enough to come to the instant aid of countries suffering from natural disasters beyond their control including famine, earthquake, fire or flood. These happen with such regularity that it would be helpful to have assistance at-the-ready when an emergency strikes.

The most important consideration is to get both the IMF and World Bank out of their coercive roles as "Enforcers" of the Trilat vision of the New World Order, and to rescind all of the conditions that have been imposed on nation states by them. The effective date could be labelled a new "D" day, short for "Democracy Day".

So, either wind up the World Bank, and use its assets for debt relief, or make it an aid institution ready to cope with disasters of the natural kind.

CHANGE THE BANKING SYSTEM

This is the key to any real hope for a world of justice and opportunity for all. As long as nearly all new money is created as debt, the world economy cannot and will not grow fast enough to accommodate the legitimate needs of its people. And the distribution of income between lenders and borrowers will widen the giant gulf which can never be bridged. A better vision is one that tends to close the gap, or at least keep it from widening.

What I am proposing is the total elimination of all Third World external debt, and most of the foreign debt of those European countries still struggling to effect the transition from state-capitalism to a privately-administered capitalist system. The write-off would include all of the money owed to the IMF, the World Bank, Regional Development Banks, individual country loans and private bank loans to debtor governments. To the extent that this would require reimbursement to third parties, including the redemption of World Bank bonds, for example, it would be paid for by the world's richest countries in an amount proportional to each country's year 2000 GDP in U.S. dollars, as a percentage of total GDP, in U.S. dollar equivalent, for that list of countries. The United States would be the largest contributor. Other major donors would include Japan, Germany, France, Italy, the U.K. and Canada. The Scandinavian countries, and some of the smaller European countries including Switzerland, as well as Australia and New Zealand, would also want to be included on the list as a matter of principle.

The whole operation would be paid for by the simple expedient of increasing the cash reserve requirements of private banks and other deposit-taking institutions by 1% a month until enough cash had been created to pay off the debt. The whole operation wouldn't take more than a couple of years. At that point industrialized countries would have the option of continuing the process until the reserve requirement reached 50% of deposits, or whether to achieve this level over a more extended period.

In *Stop: Think*, in conjunction with the widely proclaimed Year of the Jubilee, a reference to the Biblical practice of debt forgiveness every 50 years, I recommended increasing cash reserves by 1% a month until they reach 50%, the same ratio as when the Bank of England was first chartered. This means that in the United States, where total deposits are roughly of the same magnitude as the $5.6 trillion dollar federal debt, a 50% reserve requirement, achieved over a period of about five years, would allow the creation of approximately $2.8 trillion of legal tender. The first trillion would be roughly the U.S. share of world debt reduction, leaving the balance available to reduce U.S. federal debt by about $1.8 trillion. That amount of debt relief would save taxpayers $75 to $85 billion in annual interest charges, which would help to offset some of the reduced revenue resulting from lower taxes.

IS DEBT FORGIVENESS JUST?

It depends on your point of view. There are those who insist that all debt should be repaid. Sounds great, but it is impossible. Debt is being created at a faster rate than the ability to repay it. So some of it has to be written off through bankruptcies and defaults. In Canada, for example, total federal, provincial, municipal, corporate and personal debt is almost $2 trillion, whereas the GDP is just a little over $1 trillion. But the average interest rate on the debt is much higher than the average growth rate of the economy. So only part of the debt can be repaid unless much of it is monetized – a fact which those people obsessed with debt reduction should keep in mind.

So the question arises, if some debt is going to be reduced or eliminated through monetization, whose debt should it be? The answer raises the question of equity and fairness. It would appear that the beneficiaries should be taxpayers in general, and Third World countries in particular. They comprise the poorest people on earth and consequently are most in need of financial relief.

In the course of researching this book I had lunch with an investment banker whose response to this suggestion was that if we paid off their debt they would only do it all over again. I could have anticipated his reply because it is an automatic one. It is the one that is passed from mouth to mouth with little or no debate and, frankly, I don't believe it. Some of the creditors, like the IMF and World Bank, would no longer exist, and consequently, would not be in a position to repeat the errors they had made in promoting bad loans.

Private creditors would be so relieved to get their capital back that they would be very reluctant to get themselves into the same jam again. Any new loans would depend on the soundness of the government and the validity of the project, which are criteria that should apply to sound banking but which were not applied in the case of much of the existing debt.

Most important, there would be little need for Third World borrowing. If the present debt were eliminated they could use their earnings from exports to finance their own needs rather than paying most of it in interest to their foreign creditors. Inevitably there would be some exceptions to the good governance rule, but they would be on their own and the citizens of each country would have to deal with their bad governors by one means or another.

My point is that the industrial North has played a major part in the penury of the South and has a responsibility to acknowledge the fact and make amends. For example, the World Bank cannot escape part of the responsibility. It actively sought projects to finance and encouraged large-scale borrowing. It was like taking kids to the candy store and telling them they could have anything they liked. The rub came later when they realized that they were obliged to pay the candy store owner out of their meagre allowance. The tragedy was compounded by the fact that many of the projects were not self-liquidating. The easy money was spent but the debt remained.

Nor can the monetarist and neo-classical economists escape responsibility. It was the implementation of their views that pushed interest rates to intolerable heights which resulted in debt compounding several times faster than any reasonable borrower might have expected. What happened was a complete reversal of the trickle-down theory of economics. Every increase in interest rates became the equivalent of an extra tax on the poorest members of society for the benefit of their rich creditors.

Western governments have a responsibility for allowing this to happen. They allowed Third World countries to be inundated with debt and then adopted interest rate policies that converted a very bad situation into one that is totally impossible. So a good case can be made that Third World debt was the product of misdirected altruism, very bad economics, greed and subterfuge on the part of the First World. It is quite justifiable in the circumstances to invoke *force majeure*. Let the people and institutions primarily responsible for the disaster accept the consequences and set the situation right.

The United States itself set a precedent in respect of Odious Debt when it repudiated Cuba's debts after Spain "lost" Cuba in the Spanish American War. As Patricia Adams, author of *Odious Debts*, put it in an interview with Julliette Majot: "The repudiation was based on the grounds that Spain had borrowed the money without the consent of the Cuban people and had used the money to suppress the Cubans' legitimate rebellion against Spain's colonial rule. The legal scholar who coined the phrase 'the doctrine of odious debts', Alexander Sack, also said that debts incurred to subjugate a people or to colonize them should also be considered odious to the indigenous people."[2]

I have long argued that there is a very fine line, and often none at all, between morality and enlightened self-interest. Paying off Third World and developing country debt qualifies on both counts. The world will benefit, as a result, both politically and economically. As long as the debt remains we are sitting on a powder keg. New loans are required just to pay the interest on existing debt. The IMF is using taxpayers money to make it appear that the loans are performing, when in reality they are not. Meanwhile, the principal amount of the debt continues to grow. The shell game can't go on forever, so it is better to do something now before the whole financial system collapses like a deck of cards.

THE WTO MUST GO

It may seem a little bit ironic that just at the moment when an effort is being made to admit China to the World Trade Organization, in an effort to get it to abide by the Trilat rules, someone should seriously suggest that it has already outlived its usefulness. There are two profound objections which can only be remedied by striking down the WTO and retracing our steps to the point at which it was born.

One of the WTO's objectives, as Sylvia Ostry constantly reminds us, is a rules-based trade regime. That sounds reasonable, but surely not just one set of rules applying to all countries. The World Boxing Federation has fifteen classes including flyweight, lightweight, middleweight and heavyweight. I would guess that the world's many different countries could be classified in as many as fifteen different categories. Certainly, not just one! As I mentioned earlier, the WTO rules were written by or on behalf of heavyweights for the benefit of heavyweights. The result is a trade regime under which everyone else is going to get clobbered.

The second objection is the loss of democracy. The WTO exercises *de facto* executive, judicial and legislative powers equivalent to that of a world government. These powers were transferred to it without the advice or consent of the peoples affected. Apologists for the WTO say that consent was granted when people elected the governments which did the deal. But that is a cop-out. The governments neither told their electors what was involved nor asked their opinion about it. Needless to say this was deliberate policy on the part of governments attempting to serve two masters.

The resulting loss of sovereignty is not acceptable. It is extremely offensive that the rights and prerogatives of nation states should be decided by unelected, unaccountable three-person panels. How does that square with the concept of democracy? It doesn't! It is all part of the plot to end popular democracy as we used to know it, and substitute a corporate plutocracy in its stead. Everything that men and women fought and died for is being taken away by stealth.

The only satisfactory remedy is to abolish the WTO and go back to the General Agreement on Tariffs and Trade from which it sprang. From there we can build a trade regime which preserves the essential powers of nation states, recognizes the different needs of countries based on size, population and state of development, and provides the flexibility for cooperative rather than coercive relationships. For want of a better description I call them the Marquis of Queensberry Rules for Trade.

THE MARQUIS OF QUEENSBERRY RULES FOR TRADE

- Fair trade, not "free trade". There is no such thing as genuine free trade as Canada has found in its relationship with the U.S.
- Every country should have the right to protect some of its infant industries. If it doesn't, they will never grow to adult-hood.
- Every country has the right to determine the conditions under which direct foreign investment is welcome.
- Every country has the right to impose controls on the movement of short-term capital in cases of emergency.
- Every country has the right to determine the limits of foreign ownership in each area of economic activity.
- Every nation state should have the right to decide what trade concessions it will put on the table in exchange for others as was the case under the GATT.
- Every country should have control over its own banking system including majority ownership.

- Every country has the right to use its own central bank to assist in the financing of essential services and to keep the economy operating at or near its potential at all times.
- Rich countries should be encouraged to license the use of their technology by poor countries at modest cost.
- Every country should be obligated to cooperate with other countries in the protection of the oceans, their species, the ozone layer and in all ways essential to protect the ecosystem for the benefit of future generations.
- Every country should be encouraged to maintain some control over its own food supply, to the extent practical, and not become dependent on patented seeds and products.
- Every country should have the right, and should be encouraged, to develop and maintain a significant degree of self-sufficiency in the production of goods and services for the use and enjoyment of its own people and in order to reduce its vulnerability to the vagaries of decisions made by people far away who might be inclined to view foreigners more in the context of economic digits rather than as human beings.

A friend who read these rules made the following notation. "You are urging the elimination of some of the major international institutions, the IMF, World Bank, and World Trade Organization, and a return to the 'protectionist' world of the past. Is this really a good idea?"

To him, and others, may I say that is not what I am recommending. What I am proposing is the transformation of a system which is immoral and inefficient, into one that is fundamentally moral and much more efficient – a system where everyone, everywhere, can hope for better things to come.

The New World Order is a greed-driven monster which gains credibility from an economic theory based on academic abstractions far removed from the real world and real people. Classical economics is a numbers game, in which people are digits. They are counted, sorted, exploited when useful, and abandoned when surplus. It would be numerically inefficient to treat them otherwise.

I am proposing a system where human beings are entitled to a status greater than inanimate objects – one where they will have some control over their own lives and destiny. Such a system would be closer to the model of nature, where babies and children are protected until they reach maturity and can compete on their own. Even then, there are physical and intellectual differences between adults that must be taken into account.

This brings me to the question of "free trade". I have always been a free trader at heart, because that is what I learned at college. One of my earliest speeches in the House of Commons was to propose free trade world-wide to be achieved over a period of fifty years by reducing tariffs at the rate of 2% each year. The assumption, of course, was that in fifty years all economies would be sufficiently developed that they could trade as equals.

Of course I was naïve to believe that this would happen. Today I am older and wiser, and I know that my assumption was wrong. Today, I understand that nation states are more like the three bears, papa bear, mama bear, and baby bear. Papa bear needs no protection. He is big and strong and can look after himself. Mama bear needs only a little bit of protection, while baby bear is in need of a lot.

Canada, for example, can compete with the U.S. in manufacturing. We have proven that, so no protection is needed. We cannot, however, compete in dairy and poultry products and never will be able to because the differences in scale are too great. So if we want to maintain some control over our own food supply, we will have to continue to provide some protection for our farmers.

We have other concerns to think about. Canada is blessed with abundant supplies of energy and water. We are already sharing one, and are coming under increasing pressure to share the other. Under NAFTA, however, if we start selling water to the U.S. we can't turn it off, even if circumstances demanded. Also the day might come when we would prefer to use these resources as an inducement to encourage industry, with its high-value-added, to locate here, rather than encouraging the flight of industry, and jobs, to warmer climes.

Our problems are nothing, however, compared to those of poor and developing countries. In many cases they have little to trade except, perhaps, a single commodity like cocoa, coffee, or rubber. Prices of these commodities are very volatile and are usually too low to pay for high-value-added manufactured products from the First World. So they simply must be able to restrict imports and develop domestic industries in some variety. Otherwise they are sentenced to perpetual poverty.

So the Marquis of Queensberry Rules are designed to give back to people much of the decision-making power that has been taken away from them by the IMF, the World Bank and the WTO in their effort to install a single, homogeneous system worldwide. An analogy I like is that the Marquis of Queensberry Rules are designed to permit "tailor-made" solutions to fit the need of individual countries, rather than the "one size fits all," which really means that it doesn't fit anyone properly.

The new system would begin with a resurrected GATT, and carry on from there, but without the WTO. As before, each country would put something on the table in exchange for advantages from others. But each would be able to withhold items appropriate to its own individual circumstances. What individual countries could not do is have it both ways. They could not dominate export markets, as Japan did for a number of years, and still protect most of their domestic industries. The object of the exercise is equity and not single country advantage.

To do that requires a change in the most favoured nation (MFN) rule to recognize the immense disparity in the power and wealth of nations. Poor and developing countries should be more heavily favoured than the rich and powerful. As in other areas of international commerce, it is impossible to have one rule which is equally just for all.

If the Marquis of Queensberry Rules, including the right of nation states to use their own central banks to finance internal development, were put into effect world economic growth would accelerate sharply. The system would be markedly more efficient. It would engage millions of people now sitting idly on the sidelines in the process of improving their own circumstances and those of their compatriots.

It would also be much more moral. The New World Order is intrinsically evil because it marginalizes people and countries to the point of despair. One of the reasons for the incredible turnout of young protestors at the G8 summit in Genoa in July, 2001, was the high youth unemployment rate in that city. Young people without hope are driven to desperate measures They heard world leaders talk about how next year they will address poverty in Africa but their words had a hollow ring, because it is all tokenism. Consequently, the protestors think their leaders are disconnected from the real world, so they take to the streets.

I definitely do not condone violent protest. It detracts from the tens of thousands of non-violent protestors who feel passionately about the future of the world. But I can understand how things get out of hand when emotions run so deep. Assurances from world leaders appear reminiscent of the "Let them eat cake" that was the final straw leading to the French revolution.

Martin Luther King, Jr. was very perceptive when he said: "There is nothing more dangerous than to build a society, with a large segment of people in that society, who feel they have no stake in it; who feel that they have nothing to lose. People who have a stake in their society, protect that society, but when they don't have it, they unconsciously want to destroy it." He may have had America in mind when he said that, but it applies equally to the world. The better vision is one where everyone is involved, everyone is contributing, everyone is benefitting, and everyone has something worth protecting. The good news is that such a world is possible. The vision of a happier, healthier, better educated and more productive world can be made real.

CHAPTER 11

MISTER PRESIDENT

"A friend is someone who tells you the truth."

George W. Bush[1]

If that is your definition, Mr. President, I guess I qualify as one of your friends because I intend to state the truth as I see it. That is not to say that you will be pleased, however, because I have known several politicians with much authority who said they wanted friends to level with them but who were less than thrilled when the invitation was accepted.

To begin, I must admit that I wondered whose friend you were when you abruptly announced that the U.S. would not adhere to the Kyoto Protocol. Could it be that you were influenced by the oil industry with which you and your family have had such a long and close connection? That suspicion was reinforced when you said you would permit exploration in the highly sensitive Arctic National Wildlife Reserve in Alaska. You must know that the drilling would be concentrated in the small calving area used by the Porcupine caribou, and that this would threaten the herd of more than 130,000 animals upon which the region has depended for centuries.

I was even more concerned when your Vice President, Dick Cheney, came to Toronto in early May, 2001, and told the annual meeting of the Associated Press that to ask Americans to conserve energy or place faith in alternative fuels will take a back seat to old standbys like oil, natural gas, coal and more nuclear power.[2]   Many of my compatriots were equally concerned about this because they feel that preserving the world ecosystem for the benefit of future generations is not only advisable, but absolutely essential.   For the U.S. to exempt itself from this responsibility, and to leave the concern to others, is not the mark of world leadership.   The fossil fuel industry may consider you its friend but you appear to have disqualified yourself as a friend of the Earth.

The problem seems to be your sense of priorities. Instead of being primarily concerned about the poor of your country, and the countless millions in other countries who do not have enough food to eat and water to drink, and preserving the planet so that their children, hopefully, will have a chance for a better life, your principal concerns include commerce and defence – neither of which will provide any comfort to those most in need.   This quandary leads to the thorny question of who is really running the United States, anyhow?

THE TWO U.S. GOVERNMENTS – PERMANENT AND PROVISIONAL

The idea of a "permanent government" is not new, but Lewis Lapham, editor of *Harper's* magazine, summed it up well in one sentence as part of his 'On Politics, Culture and the Media' keynote address to the Canadian Institute of International Affairs national foreign policy conference, in October, 1996. His definition: "The permanent government is the secular oligarchy that comprises the Fortune 500 companies and all their attendant lobbyists, the big media and entertainment syndicates, the civil and military services, the larger research universities and law firms."[3]

That pretty well sums it all up in a way that conforms with my sense of the real politic.   The big transnational corporations with their lobbyists, public relations firms and lawyers, the international banks with their close ties to both the FED and the Treasury Department, not to mention the IMF and World Bank, the close, almost incestuous relationship between Bretton Woods institutions and the State Department, the information conglomerates that blur the lines between the manufacture of news, and culture and its dissemination. These are all parts of the permanent government that hold the reins of real power. It is a power camouflaged by the antics of the politicians comprising the provisional government.

Lapham puts it in historical context. "Just as the Catholic church was the predominant institution in medieval Europe, and the Roman legion the most efficient manifestation of organized force in the 1st and 2nd centuries BC, so also the transnational corporation arranges the affairs of the late 20th [and early 21st] century. The American Congress and the American President serve at the pleasure of their commercial overlords, all of whom hold firmly to the belief that all government regulation is wicked (that is, the work of the Devil) and that any impulse that runs counter to the manly interest of business is, by definition, soft, effeminate and liberal.

"On behalf of the corporations that pay the campaign money, the politicians collect taxes in the form of handsome subsidies and congenial interest rates. The president performs the duties of a mendicant friar – sympathetic to the sufferings of the peasantry, but alert to the concerns of the lords and nobles. Fortunately for the domestic tranquility of the United States, the American political system allows for the parallel sovereignty of two governments, one permanent and the other provisional.

"The permanent government ... hires the country's politicians and sets the terms and conditions under which the citizenry can exercise its right – God-given but increasingly expensive – to life, liberty and the pursuit of happiness. Obedient to the rule of men, not laws, the permanent government oversees the production of wealth, builds cities, manufactures goods, raises capital, fixes prices, shapes the landscape, and reserves the right to speak to the customers in the language of low motive and base emotion.

"The provisional government is the spiritual democracy that comes and goes on the trend of the political season and oversees the production of pageants. It exemplifies the nation's moral aspirations, protects the citizenry from unworthy or unholy desires, and devotes itself to the mending of the American soul. Positing a rule of laws instead of men, the provisional government must live within the cage of high-minded principle, addressing its remarks to the imaginary figure known as the thinking man, a superior being who detests superficial reasoning and quack remedies, never looks at *Playboy*, trusts Bill Moyers [public TV], worries about political repression in Liberia, reads (and knows himself improved by it) the op-ed page of the *Wall Street Journal.*"[4]

So there you have it, Mr. President, the root cause of my concern. I think you listen to the wrong people. You were at the Summit of the Americas in Québec City in April 2001. You saw all the ruckus that took place there and most of your advisers couldn't figure out what the protest was all about. In a word, it was because we thought your role was that of a paid "actor" reading the script written for you by the transnational corporations and international banks which comprise such a powerful element in your permanent government.

It didn't help one little bit that our Prime Minister, Jean Chrétien, was reading from the same script written, or copied, by our permanent government. To hear the two of you talk about "Free Trade" and "Democracy" without a word of explanation that what you really meant was unrestricted investment and corporate rule, was enough to bring tears to the eyes. They say that only good actors can succeed in politics, and the two of you were so convincing that many of my friends actually took your words literally. Some even said nice things about you, editorially.

The protesters who were outside the fence at Québec City, the ones who were subjected to tear gas and rubber bullets, were less generous in their reviews. They believe that what was really going on inside the fence was a well orchestrated plan to open up all of South and North America to exploitation by transnational corporations and international banks, most of which are American. Their benefits will be guaranteed by unrestricted access and by a disputes settlement mechanism similar to Chapter 11 of NAFTA, which allows them to contest laws passed by local governments. The benefits promised to the small countries and their people are largely fictional.

So you see, Mr. President, there are a lot of people, including millions of your fellow Americans, who think you have got your priorities all wrong. There is already enough wealth in the United States to eliminate poverty totally. Yet when you define poverty as anyone earning less than 40% of the average income, your poverty rate is above 10%, one of the highest in the industrialized world.

A couple of years ago, when I was writing another book, I checked and found that according to U.S. federal statistics a worker earning the minimum $5.15 an hour would have to work an estimated 88 hours a week to afford a one-bedroom in Miami, while in Westchester County, N.Y., a minimum wage earner would have to work 150 hours a week to afford an average priced two-bedroom apartment. Doesn't that strike you as a little bit ridiculous in the richest country in the world?

The problem, as you well know, is the distribution of income. In 1973, just before your permanent government and its cohorts in other countries including ours, changed the whole economic system in favour of monetarism, as preached by Milton Friedman and his Chicago School, the richest 10% of American families with children made 21 times more than the poorest ten percent. By 1996, the richest 10% made 314 times more than the poorest.[5] The policies that you were pushing at Québec City are designed to guarantee that this trend continues both in your country and other countries including, regrettably, Canada.

Some of your top business types, members of your permanent government, have become unspeakably greedy. A Reuters dispatch from New York in May, 1998, quoted *Forbes* magazine to the effect that Travelers Group chairman, Sanford Weill, received $228 million in compensation in 1997 – more than George Lucas, Oprah Winfrey or Michael Jordan – making him the highest-paid boss in the United

States. Behind Weill on the list were insurer Conseco's CEO
Stephen Hilbert, with $125 million, HealthSouth Corp's
Richard Scrushy, $107 million, Occidental Petroleum Corp's
Ray Irani, $105 million and industrial powerhouse Allied
Signal Inc's Lawrence Bossidy, $58 million.[6]

This kind of intellectual and moral rot is spreading
from the U.S. around the world like a virulent virus. "'The
rest of the world is moving to our pay model,' said Kevin J.
Murphy, a University of Southern California finance
professor and a leading expert on worldwide executive pay.
Maybe that movement is out of efficiency, maybe it is out of
greed – we don't know which it is yet – but the trend is
clear.'"[7]

The answer to the question is really obvious. No
person, regardless of how efficient he or she may be, is
worth that much money for a year's work. Oh I know that
there have been cases of a turnaround that justify a good
reward. But too often the prize is given to those who
negotiate takeovers or mergers that result in serious
downsizing. A few thousand people lose their jobs and the
person responsible takes home a bag of gold.

While a case can be made for rewards based on
performance, the corporate culture has disintegrated to the
point where CEOs get enormous farewell gifts when their
contribution to a company has been neutral or negative. In
the spring of 2001, it became clear that Ed Tyler, the CEO of
Moore Corporation, an international company that just
happens to be based in Canada, should bite the executive
dust. The board of directors decided to replace him, but
made his departure sweet with a going away gift package of
US$26.5 million, after a disappointing 20 month reign that
saw about US$1.2 billion evaporate from the firm's market
value.[8] Shareholders, who of course were not consulted,
were appropriately outraged.

So you can understand, Mr. President, why protesters
feel the system is all askew. Not only is there ample wealth
in the U. S. – and Canada too – to eliminate poverty quickly
and permanently if that were the number one priority of your
government, there is already enough wealth and expertise in

the world to ensure that every person had access to the basic essentials of food, potable water, clothing, shelter, education and health care within a decade. Admittedly it would be a monumental task. It would require the same kind of dedication and concentration that was required to put the first man on the moon, for example, but it could be done and all of the necessary tools are available.

The reason it is not likely to be done is because it is not on the agenda. You and your G8 colleagues talked about African poverty in Genoa, in July 2001, but the elimination of poverty worldwide is so far down on the priority list that it is not visible to the naked eye. The political will that is a prerequisite to action does not exist. Neither your government, nor the permanent government of the U.S., has it on the radar screen. Both are preoccupied with projects like the National Missile Defense System and extending economic domination under the guise of a New World Order.

With your unilateral decision to proceed with the National Missile Defense (NMD), you managed to alienate the vast majority of thinking persons. Wilson Riles of the American Friends Service Committee, a think-tank, spoke for many when he said, "The Bush administration has stepped up the search for another enemy. This does not bode well for the needs of U.S. citizens." Indeed it doesn't. It doesn't bode well for anyone except the few people who will benefit directly.

I am not going to repeat all the arguments against the NMD here. But your reasons for proceeding are a straw man if I ever saw one. There are other, better ways of dealing with rogue states than to start a new cold war. You know as well as I do how these things work. You will start with a shield designed to protect against one or two missiles only. But that will be enough to unnerve other states like Russia and China, and the arms race will be underway again. At that stage you will conclude that only a massive shield will protect the U.S., and a desperate effort will be made to get into the position where you could strike first, as a pre-emptive measure.

That kind of "thinking", which is routine at the Pentagon, is not only morally monstrous, it is dangerously deceptive. A few of your top military advisers have been hit with the Maginot Line virus. You may be too young to remember what that was, but as I have actually seen it, perhaps I should explain. After World War I, French generals decided to build a solid line of impregnable fortresses along the German border. The magnificent big guns, all pointing in the direction from which an attack would occur, would keep the enemy at bay and allow the French to relax and sleep well.

That was the theory. It is exactly the same one you are using to justify the NMD. But when the Germans did decide to attack, they didn't play the French game. They just drove their armoured divisions around the Maginot Line which proved to be worse than useless. That is exactly what rogue states would do if they really wanted to get you. They wouldn't attack with long range missiles. They would use cargo ships to move atomic bombs into U.S. port cities. Or they would launch extremely light, manned or robot planes, too small to be detected on your radar screens, but large enough to carry small atomic bombs or canisters of deadly germs – like the ones your country has been developing.

In your inaugural address you said: "We will build our defences beyond challenge, lest weakness invite challenge."[9] Those are brave words, Mr. President, but what you are promising is impossible. The reality is that there is no such thing as security in today's world, and there never again will be. So to suggest otherwise is really misleading. Which brings me to the even greater mystery of why your country would be planning to spend additional billions to put guns in space.

Your Defense Secretary, Donald H. Rumsfeld, sent a letter to Congress in May in which he addressed the issue of potential offensive actions in space. "The Department of the Air Force will be assigned responsibility to organize, train and equip for prompt and sustained offensive and defensive space operations," Rumsfeld wrote, in explaining how he wants to reorganize the Defense Department's approach to managing national security space activities such as satellite operations. When a reporter noted that Rumsfeld included the term "offensive" space operations, Lt.-Gen. Robert Foglesong, deputy chief of staff for air and space operations, replied, "Potentially that."[10]

Just who is it that you plan to take on for size in space, Mr. President, the Martians? Who or what could possibly justify such extravagance? Is this just another case of the military-industrial establishment that a former Republican president, General Eisenhower, warned about actually calling the shots? Or are there really some Unidentified Flying Objects that we haven't been told about flying around up there?

AMERICAN VALUES

I guess what really distresses me is the discordance between the words and the music. In your inaugural address you said: "And to all nations, we will speak for the values that gave our nation birth."[11] You speak about them, but do you practise them? That is the line that Ambassador Richard Holbrook was using when he was advocating bombing Yugoslavia. Not only did the U.S. have a responsibility to intervene in world hot-spots, there was also a necessity for America to "stand up for its values". So the whole operation against Belgrade was wrapped in a moral cloak of extremely doubtful authenticity. If ever there was an unnecessary war, it was that one which had an unhealthy overtone of commercialism.

So what are American values? I always note that you still put "In God We Trust" on your coins. But surely that is just for old time's sake. If you forget the words and look at the reality your gods are power and money. And you don't appear to be too willing to share these, either within your own country, or with others less fortunate. Your tendency toward unilateral decisions in foreign policy such as your determination to proceed with the NMD and your rejection of the Kyoto Protocol is deeply offensive to friend and foe alike. Of equal concern are your spending priorities at home and your relentless pursuit of "Free Trade" protocols designed for the benefit of American "interests" on the world stage.

The American dream is alive and well for the bright, the well-educated, the lucky and those who are born rich. For many others, the relative poverty is increasing. And for those too poor or too unlucky to have adequate health insurance, severe illness can turn their dream of better times to come into the nightmare of financial ruin. So what were these unfortunate people thinking when they heard you say these stirring words: "The grandest of these ideals is an unfolding American promise that everyone belongs, that everyone deserves a chance, that no insignificant person was ever born." [12]

INSIDIOUS IMPERIALISM

The United States earned near universal admiration after World War II when it insisted that the European Imperial Powers grant freedom to their colonies. One after another, the former colonies were granted their fondest wish and became free at last. I still remember the sense of euphoria and the dancing in the streets as the old Imperial flags were lowered and the new flags of Independence went up in their place.

Little did anyone dream at the time that within two generations these same countries would be re-colonized to an extent previously deemed impossible. For a while, the newly independent countries had been able to exercise a considerable element of freedom as a result of the cold war. Competition between the U.S. and the Soviet Union, which President Ronald Reagan later dubbed the Evil Empire, allowed leaders of the newly minted countries to play off one of the great powers against the other.

That freedom of choice began to end with the move to higher interest rates in 1980. Existing debts at variable interest rates became a straight-jacket for less developed countries. U.S. tolerance for national ambitions quickly evaporated, and the world was ripe for conquest but, for the first time in history, the conquest would not be achieved by bombs and gunboats, but by the much more subtle means of bonds and bank loans. It was inevitable that the noose of compound interest would soon turn free men into slaves.

International financial institutions like the IMF and World Bank have aided and abetted the process. Their rules and dictates are the chains and shackles that force poor countries to sit helplessly by as their resources and industries are increasingly pillaged by foreign predators – a process that will be recorded in history as one of the great crimes against humanity. Millions of innocents have died as a consequence of the economic strangulation.

What is impossible to explain is how the United States could be a party to such inhumanity. No doubt some of the apparent indifference is due to lack of knowledge of the plight of the poor – the real world apart from the cozy one most powerful Americans know. Perhaps your responsibility, Mr. President, is to make them more aware of what the U.S. is really doing. Meanwhile this Libertarian, me first, philosophy is worrisome. It is reminiscent of the late 19th century when men like John D. Rockefeller, Sr. were alleged to have prayed on their knees on Sunday, and preyed on the people the other six days of the week. And part of my concern is that these ideas have spread northward into my country where they have wreaked political and economic havoc on a scale unknown to my generation. Some Canadians appear to be quite willing to sell Canada to the highest bidder.

Canada had barely escaped from the yoke of British colonialism when it began to fall under the spell of the United States. Frankly, we needed your help to industrialize and establish ourselves as a self-respecting, independent country. Everything went extremely well for a while and we all thought we were going to live happily ever after. But then two things went wrong. We adopted your economic system, the one hatched by the Chicago School, and put our economy on the skids. Our central bank was not even as successful at damage control as Alan Greenspan was in yours.

The second thing is that you didn't like the way we were running our country. You didn't think we had the right to decide which of our resources and industries were up for grabs, and which were not. So your ambassador planted some seeds in fertile minds that led first to the FTA and, then, NAFTA, which limit our ability to run our own affairs and, at the same time, give to your big industries the power to decide which of our companies they would like to buy at fire-sale prices. In the last ten years, they have bought so many that we are definitely losing control of our own destiny. We are increasingly marching to the American drum.

You can imagine my dismay, then, when I picked up the local Trilat propaganda sheet of June 30, the day before our Canada Day, and read that your new ambassador to Ottawa, Paul Cellucci, has suggested that Canada, the United States and Mexico should forge closer links as part of a "NAFTA-plus" relationship based on harmonization of border controls, law enforcement, energy, environmental and immigration policies.[13]

Now I admit that Canadians are a little bit dense, witness the fact that we let you get away with the FTA in the first place. But what the ambassador was telegraphing, loud and clear, was that we should adopt American standards in these areas, and begin the final stages of integration leading to the absorption of Canada by the U.S. It would be naïve to believe that the timing of this announcement was coincidental.

As soon as I saw the report of the ambassador's pitch I said: "The wolves are coming in for the kill." I thought of everything that has happened in the last decade or so, and recalled how the U.S has relentlessly pursued its commercial interests like a pack of wolves pursuing a deer through the snow. The deer becomes increasingly exhausted by the chase and eventually loses its will to fight on for life itself. I have seen this happen to more and more of my compatriots who increasingly see the blood drops in the snow and say the chase is almost over. The premature death of our beautiful country is increasingly inevitable.

There are still some Canadians, however, who do not want to become Americans. We prefer you in the former role of friend and neighbour. One of our well-known

Canadian politicians, the late Rt. Hon. J.W. Pickersgill, used to say that good fences make good neighbours. And there is a considerable amount of truth in that.

There are many reasons why we prefer to keep our independence, and I will list some of them in the next chapter. But one of those reasons is American values. We prefer to choose the ones that we like, *a la carte*, without being stuck with a package deal. We think you have too many of your disadvantaged people in jail, for example, and that there are too many guns flying around. But these pale in significance compared to your sense of priorities, what you think is important and what isn't.

One of your priorities, and undoubtedly the most offensive one, is the attempt to impose American values on a reluctant world. Specifically you want the world to accept and adopt your economic system, *carte blanche*, whether it is good for them or not. Your time-table for Russian "reform", for example, proved to be an unmitigated disaster. A new book entitled *The Mystery of Capital: Why Capitalism Triumphs in the West and Fails Everywhere Else*, by Hernando de Soto, explains why some species can't be instantaneously transplanted into a different environment. The essential nutrients don't exist to give them life.

And why should Washington feel obliged to tell everybody what to do? In June, 2001, the new prime minister of Japan, Junichiro Koizumi paid you a visit. You felt obliged to urge him to have Japanese banks dispose of their bad loans. Unfortunately, that is probably the worst possible advice you could give if you have any concern at all for the Japanese people. Calling those thousands of loans will result in mass bankruptcies and a big increase in unemployment which is already too high. So who needs that kind of advice which is the kind being dished out daily by mis-educated economists.

In conclusion, Mr. President, I guess my question is this: "What makes you think you have the God-given right to run the world by fiat from Washington? Especially when you are running it in the interests of a very small group of people who have bread enough and to spare, while much of the world goes hungry." I know that you have the power to do it, but do you have the right to do it? Does might make right?

What I am suggesting is that the American values of today are so far removed from those held by the founders of your great country that they are no longer compatible with the principles for which they stood. I urge you to read and reflect on the following quotation from the third president of the Republic, Thomas Jefferson, who said: "When all government, domestic and foreign, shall be drawn to Washington as the centre of all power, it will render powerless the checks provided of one government on another, and will become as venal and oppressive as the government from which we separated."

CHAPTER 12

VIVE LA DIFFERENCE

"As we enter our centennial year [1967] we are still a young nation, very much in the formative stages.   Our national condition is still flexible enough that we can make almost everything we wish of our nation.   No other country is in a better position than Canada to go ahead with the evolution of a national purpose devoted to all that is good and noble and excellent in the human spirit."

Lester B. Pearson

In my rare bad moments, I sometimes think that we Canadians don't deserve to possess such a beautiful country with so much promise. All too often we have been a bunch of wimps, sissies, opportunists, and ingrates – a totally incomprehensible *mélange* of human beings. Many of our actions over the years defy rational explanation.

In 1949 we built the first jet transport to fly in the Western Hemisphere.   On April 18, 1950, in a record-breaking 75 minute flight to New York, the Jetliner carried the first mail ever carried by a jet-powered aircraft.   Three cheers for our side.   Canadians, many of them immigrants but unabashedly Canadian, were world leaders in the field of jet aviation.   Then suddenly, and inexplicably, we cut the plane in half with an acetylene torch. Two weeks later, an American airline announced the first scheduled commercial flight and made it sound as if the plane was at once unique, and American.

A few years later, after taking time out to produce the CF-100, a jet fighter used by the Royal Canadian Air Force for air defence, the same design team that had produced the Jetliner undertook what became one of Canada's greatest achievements, the Avro Arrow. Our pride was unbounded. It was the sleekest, fastest manned object in the skies. Naysayers went out of their way to point out that the range of the prototype was less than adequate, and otherwise nit pick, but anyone familiar with the development of new aircraft, or anything else for that matter, would know that any deficiencies were quite capable of correction before production began.

After astounding the world with our achievement we learned that there were problems ahead. The cost of the project was greater than anticipated and we had difficulty persuading other countries to buy the product. The Armed Forces decided that the Arrow was consuming too much of the defence budget and advised the government to that effect. Eventually, in what was, from a national standpoint, one of the worst decisions in Canadian history, the project was cancelled.

To add insult to injury, work stopped immediately before a new, more-powerful Canadian-designed engine had been tested on the Mark V model. The blueprints for both the airplane and the engine, which had considerable commercial potential, were destroyed. The design team dispersed with many of the best engineers moving to the U.S. National Aeronautics and Space Agency (NASA).

Worst of all, the five existing test aircraft were ordered to be cut up with acetylene torches in one of the worst cases of official vandalism in history. Whoever made this decision didn't even have the good common sense to keep one copy for the Canadian Aviation Museum so that future generations of young Canadians could see how good we really were, and how far ahead of the rest of the world, including our neighbours to the South. Now, more than 40 years later, a Canadian patriot, Peter Zuuring, is trying to fit myriad pieces together in the hope of reconstructing one aircraft.

The pattern is all too familiar. When I arrived at the Defence Department they had been working for years on the development of the Bobcat, an Armoured Personnel Carrier, which was desperately needed by Canadian forces overseas. The cost of development, as is inevitably the case, exceeded the estimate. So the Treasury Board periodically reviewed the project and were so interminably slow that the American M-113 eventually overtook it, and we would have been irresponsible to proceed on our own. We were ahead but we couldn't make up our minds, and slid behind.

Our problem is a combination of not being able to make up our minds quickly, and fiscal prudence, although some will have doubts about the latter. In 1969, for example we were all ready to proceed with the development of an intense neutron generator which would be a world leader in its class. It was one of those years when proposed revenues and expenditures didn't quite match so the "frills" were cut – more precisely, those things that were forward-looking and future-oriented as opposed to the bread and butter items of the moment.

Canadians have a propensity to first move forward and then lose momentum, and fall behind. From 1964, when the Naval Board, the General Staff and the Air Staff were combined into a single Defence Staff, until 1974, Canada had the best military organization in the world. It was streamlined and efficient and the chain of command was clear and unequivocal. Admittedly, the green uniform was a mistake but that could have been easily remedied by dressing everyone in navy in the winter, khaki in the summer, and white for visiting foreign ports and other special occasions.

In 1974, however, the Trudeau government combined the military and civil headquarters into one, and all of the progress of the previous decade began to unravel. Oil and water do not mix and putting civilians in positions of direct authority over the forces was a dreadful mistake. It was too much for the military to accept, and became the excuse they needed to re-establish separate navy, army and air force headquarters outside Ottawa. Not only did this reinstate the wasteful triplication of pre-unification days, it fudged the chain of command to the point where disasters like Somalia could happen.

Now, after almost thirty years of "civilianization" of the military, and more than thirty years of under-funding, the forces are in a shambles. Morale is as low or lower than it has ever been, and even veterans are advising their relatives not to pursue a military career. Pay is a factor, but leadership and lack of equipment to do the jobs assigned is a greater factor. The Sea King helicopters, for example, came into service on my watch, and should have been replaced years ago.

The Canadian Armed Forces are not operationally fit and it was heartbreaking to hear the retiring Chief of Defence Staff, General Maurice Baril, and the Minister of National Defence, Art Eggleton, say otherwise. Instead of trying to kid us, why couldn't they have said "we are doing our best with what we have." To restore the kind of operational capability for which Canadians used to be known, two things are essential. The government has to provide enough money to keep personnel levels up to strength, and to buy the equipment essential for the jobs they are assigned to do. Second, the 1974 decision has to be reversed and the organization reinstated along the lines that existed before that time with separate civil and military headquarters.

1974 WAS A WATERSHED

The year 1974 not only marked an unhappy watershed for the Armed Forces, it was the year when we abandoned an economic system that had worked reasonably well for several decades in favour of one which has proved to be grossly inadequate. As I pointed out earlier, that was when BOC Governor Gerald Bouey adopted the ideas of Milton Friedman and his colleagues, and set Canada, in concert with the rest of the world, on a path of relative penury compared to our potential.

The small recession of 1974-75 caused a small upward blip in the federal debt but that was trivial compared to 1980-81 when Bouey went along with FED Chairman Paul

Volcker's atomic attack on everything that moved and breathed. The mushroom cloud of debt resulting from that explosion is still expanding. The whole operation could be labelled "Exhibit A" for an economic ideology where people don't count.

Mike Wilson was the Tory finance critic at the time, and he described the whole tight-money, high-interest rate policy as "insane". The irony is that ten years later, when he was minister of finance, the same Mike Wilson was out on the hustings defending BOC Governor John Crow for invoking a repeat performance. This is an absolutely classic case of how the Canadian permanent government, of which Crow was then an influential member, really run the country. It is a subject to which I will return later because they have run the Canadian Titanic into a monumental iceberg.

The government of Brian Mulroney really gave us the worst of both worlds. It allowed Crow to put the economy on the skids instead of using the BOC creatively to finance full employment and balance the budget. Then, when a weakened economy produced a big deficit, it didn't opt for belt-tightening, it chose tax increases, including the hated Goods and Services Tax (GST), instead. This was totally consistent with the new (old) economic theology being promoted by the IMF. By taxing consumption it manages to transfer more of the tax burden from the rich and the corporations to the poor consumers.

As bad as Mulroney's fiscal and monetary management was, it pales in significance to his legacy of the FTA, and then NAFTA. Signing the FTA was a complete "*volte-face*" because, at the time of the 1983 Progressive Conservative leadership campaign, he said: "Don't talk to me about free trade. That issue was decided in 1911. Free trade is a danger to Canadian sovereignty. You will hear none of it from me." In my opinion he was right in 1983, and I have been curious as to why he would change his mind on such a fundamental issue.

Consequently, I wrote to Mulroney when this book was in progress and asked him for his version of events leading to the transformation.[1] As I have not heard back from him, I will confine my observations to what I have gleaned from other sources. One of his ministers said there had been agitation from the Department of Trade, and from Gordon Ritchie, in particular. Mulroney also received a long memorandum from Simon Reisman, who later became Canada's chief negotiator, with Ritchie as his deputy.

There is no doubt that the idea originated South of the border. The American Ambassador at the time has since taken credit. He lobbied members of Canada's permanent government who then began to lobby the "provisional" one we had elected. Mulroney's close ties to the business community provided ready access and instant communication. The die was really cast by the time Mulroney and President Ronald Reagan met in Québec City and the unofficial seal occurred when the two joined in a chorus of "When Irish Eyes are Smiling."

The whole process was given an additional stamp of legitimacy when it was recommended by the Royal Commission on the Economic Union and Development Prospects for Canada, headed by former finance minister and later High Commissioner to London, Donald S. Macdonald. At the time his report was released Macdonald prophetically described free trade with the U.S. as "a leap of faith."

I believe Donald, himself a former Trilat and long-time member of the Bilderberger group, when he says that he thought at the time that we had no option. I would have come to a different conclusion, but I had not been travelling in the circles that he had been travelling in. Today, Donald is concerned, as I am, that in proposing to let foreigners buy our communications infrastructure, for example, that we are going too far and losing control over our own destiny.[2]

Indeed we are. I am probably more concerned than most of my friends and former colleagues, but that is due to the fact that I have been intimately involved in these matters for the last five years. I am convinced that the situation is desperate. Especially as the war escalates. In June, 2001, the *National Post* distributed a 12-page Trilat-Bilderberger propaganda supplement entitled "Falling Further Behind," which it labelled "A special investigation into the condition of the Canadian economy."[3] Heaven help us!

One of its feature articles, written by two convenient economists, Tom Velk and Al Riggs, rated six of Canada's prime ministers and concluded that Mulroney was the best. As soon as I saw it, I thought: "That means that Mulroney must have been the worst, or at least nose-to-nose with Chrétien for last place."

It is all part of a plan to "rehabilitate" Mulroney, and turn his image of recession, unemployment, the GST and "Free Trade" into a plus, instead of a very big minus. The rehabilitators are trying to prove, by constant repetition, that instead of being dumb policies, they were tough decisions in the long-term interests of the country. Excuse me, the Canadian people provided a more accurate rating when they reduced the PC Party to two seats in the 1993 election. That Mulroney was "taken in" by the permanent government is beyond question. But that is no excuse. The buck stopped in his office.

FROM BAD TO EQUALLY BAD, OR WORSE

I must admit that I was ecstatic when the government changed and the Chrétien Liberals took office in 1993. Their campaign booklet, Creating Opportunities, The Liberal Plan for Canada, dubbed the Red Book, was a well written document which covered most of the issues of major concern. It promised to abolish the GST and replace it with another tax that would be fairer, and less nuisance to small business.

It recognized the challenge of trading relationships with the U.S. "In 1988, Liberals opposed the Canada-United States Free Trade Agreement because it was flawed; Canada did not get secure access to the United States market. These flaws have been confirmed by the ongoing disputes and harassment over trade in steel, pork, softwood lumber, and other products since the FTA went into effect."[4] Their solution: "The FTA and NAFTA are flawed. A Liberal government will renegotiate them."[5]

Of course they kept neither of these promises, even though they had a whole chapter in the Red Book entitled "Integrity". They kept the GST intact, except to harmonize it with provincial sales taxes in Atlantic Canada. And it only took an hour or two with President Bill Clinton in the rare California air for the newly elected Chrétien to wimp out on NAFTA, and accept that it was okay with him. All of the flaws that had been so carefully set out remained intact, so the only thing that had changed was the willingness of one more Canadian prime minister to bow the knee to Caesar.

The whole record of the government has been one of capitulation to the forces of globalization and colonization. Not one foreign takeover of a Canadian company has been rejected even when the sale was clearly not in the public interest. They have removed the limit on foreign ownership of Canadian banks, and increased the limit from 10% to 20% for any single owner. They have removed the limit on foreign ownership of Petro Canada, so it, too, is on the auction block. Trade Minister Brian Tobin has already telegraphed the news that foreign ownership limits will be removed in the telecommunications industry, which I regard as profoundly contrary to Canadian interests.

It appears that the government has given up on Canada, and that their solution is to move further in the direction of annexation by the U.S. This squares with the subtle and subversive influence of the permanent government. I was horrified when our then ambassador to the U.S., Raymond Chrétien, raised the question of a customs union with the U.S. before a Washington audience. I wondered who had authorized flying such an obvious kite.

I was absolutely livid when I picked up my morning dose of high blood pressure and read on page one: "Union with U.S. on Table: PM's Advisor."[6] Public Policy Forum president, David Zussman, was quoted as saying: "Canadians in all parts of civil society should actively encourage a growing debate over new ideas, which, until a few years ago, were completely taboo in respectable Canadian society ... issues like dollarization, common perimeters and harmonization of standards."[7] Supporters of this idea only say that it would be faster to move trucks and goods across the border. They don't say that we would have to adopt U.S. immigration and customs laws, that the Americans would want to patrol our eastern, western and northern boundaries and that laws like the medical use of marijuana would be open to immediate and direct threat from them.

The old blood pressure got another boost when I read that Zussman was one of Chrétien's closest advisors and that he had formally and informally played a key role in the development of Liberal policy. "Who does he think he is," I asked myself aloud, "to suggest putting our country on the auction block." The backroom boys are at it again, I thought, it is just a few days since the new American ambassador to Canada was suggesting a NAFTA-plus which sounded almost exactly like Zussman.

And what makes Mr. Zussman think these are "new ideas"? They have been on the table, from time-to-time, for about four hundred years. But never before have they been "sold" by such a slick propaganda regime. That is the big difference. I was interested in the reaction of Michael Walker, executive director of the Fraser Institute, who said: "If there was a debate now I think the outcome is pretty clear."[8] What he is really saying is that the debate would be premature now; the "selling" is not yet sufficiently far advanced, and the conditioning not yet adequate for ready acceptance.

So on quiet reflection I think that Canadians should be grateful to David Zussman for "blurting out the truth" about the agenda of the permanent government and their Trilat cronies. We should and must have the debate now, because, as I have pointed out, it will not be long before we have passed the point of no return, after which any debate will be futile. Important companies are being sold off at a rate which is unsustainable. Either we stop it now, or Canada will soon become an empty shell.

No one seems to care, however, least of all the government. It seems to believe that shareholders have an innate right to sell to the highest bidder, no matter who that might be. At least one senior cabinet minister, listed among those who might succeed the prime minister, has expressed that view. The philosophy, imported from South of the border, is that there are no other rights than shareholder rights. I strongly disagree!

The proposition that there are no values other than shareholder values is a perversion of both equity and decency. Every corporation owes something, and some owe much, to taxpayers at large. Taxpayers pay for the education of the participants. In the vast majority of cases they install the infrastructure required for the company to get started and grow. In more cases than corporate executives care to admit, taxpayers provide direct subsidies, or guaranteed loans, or tax write-offs, or research and development benefits. I don't know of a single company that has not benefitted in more than one of these ways. So there are many stakeholders, in addition to shareholders, including employees, community and country. And in a just society, directors would be required by law to take all stakeholders into account before making a decision.

There is another, even more compelling argument. Nearly every country has a law like our Cultural Property Export and Import Act, which prohibits the sale of documents, artifacts, archeological discoveries and works of art if their rarity is such that they are considered national treasures. If that reservation applies to certain items that are considered priceless, from a national point of view, what about the essential industries and resources that collectively constitute the tangible soul of the country. Like the human body, you can only cut off so many of the individual parts before it ceases to be functional, and then dies. That, I regret to say, is what is happening to Canada.

I have often wondered about the worst case scenario. Assume that we continue along the present path until we reach the point, some years hence, when it becomes absolutely clear to even the slowest learner that we are going to lose our country. The angry response would be hard to contain. Voters would insist that the government of the day find scapegoats to blame for the tragedy. Obviously Messrs. Mulroney and Chrétien would come instantly to mind. In self defence the government would be obliged to have them arrested and charged with treason.

Their defence lawyers would be hard-pressed to assemble a plausible case. About the only one I can think of was born during the inquiry into the Walkerton, Ontario, tainted-water scandal. It was dubbed the "moron defence". No one told them that e-coli could be fatal.

So Mulroney would have to plead that Simon Reisman and Gordon Ritchie, the two principal Canadian architects of the FTA, never told him that an overdose of direct foreign investment, as prescribed by the treaty, could prove to be fatal. And Chrétien would have to plead that David Zussman, and the senior officials in foreign affairs and trade, only told him about the benefits of dismantling the border and never mentioned that it could lead to the end of Canada. If our two infamous prime ministers are not losing any sleep on this score, it would be because they know that whatever the sentence of a Canadian court, they would soon be the beneficiaries of an American presidential pardon.

REASONS WHY SOME CANADIANS WANT TO SAVE CANADA

There is some comfort in the knowledge that the darkest night is followed by the dawn. I know from my correspondence that increasing numbers of my compatriots understand and want to act positively. This is true of Canadians from all parts of the political spectrum. Even some Liberal back-benchers are becoming increasingly anxious about the direction their government is taking.

One could write a whole book about why being a Canadian is a privilege which should be guarded and preserved. Space prevents anything more than a few brief highlights, some of which may be self-evident, and a few, like our unique geography and history, that we don't spend much time thinking about.

OUR UNIQUE GEOGRAPHY

Most Canadians know that we occupy the second largest land mass in the world, exceeded only by Russia. It offers almost infinite variety, and few of us live long enough to see more than a tiny fraction of it. One of the advantages of public life is the opportunity to travel widely, and that has been one of the biggest bonuses of my career.

Although I had visited Newfoundland and Labrador several times, it was not until I went with the late Jack Pickersgill, then Minister of Transport and Member of Parliament for Bonavista Twillingate, that I saw and learned to love the fishing outports that a casual visitor seldom sees. It was the same with the other Atlantic provinces, as the local MP would drive from one small village to the next and point out those special features like the Bay of Fundy, with its world record tides, and Magnetic Hill in New Brunswick, which you have to see to believe.

The old ferry ride to Prince Edward Island is now gone but the red soil of the island is an eternal feature. A week's holiday near the birthplace of Lucy Maud Montgomery, by the sand dunes of the north shore, provided an unforgettable introduction to her world famous *Anne of Green Gables*, and other stories.

Québec is every bit as "special" as its people insist. Its unique feature, of course, is its language and culture. But these are married to its history and geography. That is where Canada, as we now know it, began. That is where European explorers first made contact with the aboriginals and claimed the land in the name of the King of France. The mighty St. Lawrence River was the highway of discovery and conquest and it remains the central and indispensable feature of Québec commerce. I must admit a long-time love affair with the city of Québec which is unique in America. I will try to erase from memory the unhappy connotations of my last visit during the Summit of the Americas.

Ontario, the province of my birth, takes second place to none in its variety, including its thousands of lakes and rivers. For me, the District of Muskoka, in the heart of the

Canadian Shield, is God's country. It was there that I witnessed the most spectacular aurora borealis of my life. The "northern lights" covered the entire sky and the colours kept changing like a giant kaleidoscope. It was awesome!

Manitoba has its own charm, while also boasting its very own inland seaport at Churchill, a city also known for its rocket launchers and polar bears. Nearby Saskatchewan, Canada's breadbasket, offers one of the largest, flattest areas of fertile land on Earth. The third of the trio, Alberta, has not only been blessed with underground treasures in its oil fields and tar sands, its attractions include the foothills of the rockies and those two jewel parks at Banff and Lake Louise.

Who can adequately describe the majesty of the Rocky Mountains. Flying across British Columbia toward that gem of a city, Vancouver, can be the thrill of a lifetime. It has no rival, except, perhaps, flying over Nunavut and the Territories at sundown. I will always remember that experience when the Task Force on Housing and Urban Development flew westward across the tundra. Looking down on the crimson light reflected from the vast expanse of snow and ice, an awestruck member from Montréal, Pierre Dansereau, said: "And the separatists would rob me of my share of this?"

OUR OWN UNIQUE HISTORY

We have our own unique history, too, although most of us are pretty well oblivious of it. From the early explorers including Cabot, Cartier, Champlain, Hudson and Thompson, to our more recent space explorers like Marc Garneau, Roberta Bondar and Chris Hadfield, we have our own story to tell. Many of us are not too familiar with our political heroes like Sir John A. Macdonald and Etienne Cartier, who brought the provinces of Nova Scotia, New Brunswick and Upper and Lower Canada together in the confederation of 1867. Other political pairs have included Baldwin and Lafontaine, and St. Laurent and Howe. Each played a part in the Canadian story.

Agnes McPhail achieved the distinction of being the first woman to be elected to the House of Commons. She paved the way for others until Ellen Fairclough became the first female cabinet minister, in John Diefenbaker's government, followed by Judy LaMarsh who was first on the Liberal side.

Many of our heroes and heroines have achieved greatness in the arts or sports. Authors including Lucy Maud Montgomery, Margaret Laurence, Margaret Atwood, Mordecai Richler, Robertson Davies, Pierre Berton, Alice Munro, Timothy Findlay, Michael Ondaatje, Gabriel Roy, Mavis Gallant, Jane Urquhart, Farley Mowat, W.O. Mitchell, and others. The Group of Seven and Emily Carr in the visual arts, and Karen Kain and Frank Augustyn in dance.

The list of movie stars, opera stars and popular singers who have made it on the world stage is so long that I gave up trying to include even the best known. But I thought as I wrote, if Canada had been part of the U.S. there would have been nowhere for them to go to become rich and famous. Similarly Americans like radio host Andy Barrie and urbanist Jane Jacobs, and thousands of other Americans who come to Canada would have had nowhere to come to.

In sport, names like Ned Hanlan, Canada's first world champion, Tom Longbolt, Barbara Ann Scott, Don Jackson, Kurt Browning, Brian Orser and Elvis Stoyko, Marilyn Bell and Cindy Nicholas, Gordie Howe, Wayne Gretzky, Maurice "The Rocket" Richard, Mario Lemieux, Paul Henderson, Bobby Howe, Donovan Bailey, and, of course, Terry Fox and Rick Hansen. These names are only representative of many more, so I apologize to those of you whose heroes have not been mentioned. The original list was much too long to fit the space available.

It is often said that Canadian history is dull because we have not had a civil war. A quick rejoinder might be, who needs one? But we have had our rebels. Louis Joseph Papineau defied executive authority and threatened open rebellion in Lower Canada. In Upper Canada, William Lyon Mackenzie put together a band of disparate farmers who took up arms to fight for responsible government and against the

Family Compact, that elite group that ran the province for its own exclusive benefit. You can stand in downtown Toronto in the place where one of his followers, of doubtful guilt, was hung. Mackenzie's story is particularly relevant because the situation at the time had certain similarities to the one existing today.

In wartime we have had many heroes. In the war of 1812-14 the names of Sir Isaac Brock and Joseph Brant come to mind. Air Ace Billy Bishop is a favourite from World War I. That was the war when Canadians won historic battles at Passchendaele, Amiens and Vimy Ridge, when Canada came of age as a country. With that behind us it was not surprising that in World War II Canadian sailors, soldiers and airmen, male and female, fought so courageously and well in the Battle of the Atlantic, the Battle of Britain, and on the ground from Sicily to Normandy to Holland, where Canadian soldiers were received as liberating heroes.

While this book was being written I heard a teacher tell about taking his class to Ottawa for a familiarization tour. En route, some of the students were saying that Canada sucks. Several said that the Canadian Armed Forces suck. The language was not music to my ears! When they arrived in the capital they visited the parliament buildings, went to the top of the Peace Tower, and then went to visit the Canadian War Museum.

For many it was the highlight of the trip. They were so impressed with the important role that Canada had played in two world wars that their attitude about their country changed dramatically. An added bonus was to see the tunic Sir Isaac Brock wore at the Battle of Queenston Heights, complete with the hole made by the bullet that killed him. It is a pity that we tell our young people so little about the history of their country. Most of them would love to know.

OUR OWN FOREIGN POLICY – SOMETIMES

The right to establish our own foreign policy is one of the priceless advantages of independence. Sometimes we act wisely, and sometimes we do not. But the decision is ours.

We entered World War I, in support of the United Kingdom, long before the Americans allowed themselves to be drawn into the war. We did exactly the same thing in World War II, although Prime Minister Wm. Lyon Mackenzie King held off declaring war for a week in order to demonstrate our independence from the mother country.

We played an important role in the establishment of the North Atlantic Treaty Organization in order to provide stability in Europe in the face of the Soviet threat. Later we voluntarily joined the North American Air Defence Command (later Aerospace) in order to cooperate with the Americans in the joint defence of our skies. These decisions appeared to be in our own best interest and there was general, though not universal, agreement to that effect.

Where our foreign policy diverged sharply from that of the U.S. was the Vietnam War. The U.S. wanted at least one of its friends to participate so it could be called an allied force, as was the case in Korea, some years earlier. But Canada steadfastly said no, which reflected the opinion of the vast majority of Canadians. There were many Americans who felt similarly, and we opened our borders to significant numbers of U.S. citizens who refused to fight in a war they were convinced was morally wrong. Many years later Robert McNamara, who was defense secretary at the time, admitted that he was wrong and the dissenters were right.

More recently Canada has participated in two wars that were really none of its business. The Gulf War in defence of Kuwait, was all about oil. As one American commentator aptly put it, "Do you think we would have gone to war if Kuwait's principal export had been broccoli?" The war in Yugoslavia was even more questionable. It could have been avoided until the U.S. took sides in the dispute and decided to bomb Serbia on the basis of high morality. The fact that much of the evidence used in justification of such a high-handed operation was faked, is just now coming to light.[9]

Two initiatives Canada has supported without U.S. approval or compliance have been the much-hailed land mines treaty, in which our Minister of Foreign Affairs, Lloyd

Axworthy, played such a prominent part, and the establishment of a war crimes tribunal.   In both cases Canada's influence was considerable and there would have been no way that we could have taken this independent stance had we been part of the U.S.

Canada has often played a significant middle-power role on the world stage and this is one of the many benefits that accrue to the world community as long as we have the right to speak for ourselves.   All of that would be lost if we were annexed by the United States and the world would be poorer for it.

THE FRENCH FACT

Canada's French heritage is an important part of its uniqueness.   Québec is the bastion of the French language and culture in North America, and determined to keep it that way.   One can sympathize with the goal, but as I have pointed out to many federal and provincial politicians from that province, their drive for independence is the wrong strategy.   It has been overtaken by time and globalization. Today, if the goal is to preserve their language and culture for future generations, they can only achieve their aspirations as a strong member of the Canadian family.

Most Canadians are unaware that without the French-speaking people and the aboriginals, there would be no Canada today. They were the ones who tipped the balance in 1776, and again in 1812-14. They opted for Canada because they thought their chances for cultural survival were better here than they would be as part of the U.S. Had they decided differently, both Canada and Québec would now be footnotes to history.

I realize that it has not been easy for them, and I can understand Premier Bernard Landry's resentment at the way they were treated when he was young. I know from my own experience in Ottawa in the '50s and '60s that there was no such thing as genuine equality. Nearly all of the good jobs were held by unilingual English-speaking Canadians and the aspirations of Québecers were clearly limited in scope. They could hope to be Minister of Justice, for example, but certainly not Minister of Finance, Trade, or Defence.

All of that has changed dramatically. Just as Jean LeSage and the Quiet Revolution opened the door for René Lévesque and the sweeping changes that have occurred in Québec, Mike Pearson gave Pierre Trudeau the chance to transform Ottawa. Now Québec businesses, previously dominated by the English, are dominated by the French. And a large number of the senior positions in the federal civil service are occupied by bilingual personnel of French origin.

Indeed, there are politicians from Western Canada who insist that it is impossible for their constituents to obtain meaningful employment in the federal service. They have not had the opportunity to become sufficiently proficient in French to qualify. This is a valid concern, so a little over a decade ago I proposed what I called "The Thirty Year Solution". One course in the other official language would be taught in each grade beginning with kindergarten the first year, extended to grade one the second year, and so on until grade twelve. By then students would be able to converse in either language with enough facility to qualify for any job from postal clerk to prime minister or chief of the defence staff. That would be the kind of genuine equality that exists in principle, but not in reality.

The bottom line is very clear. If Québec should separate from Canada, it would constitute a double suicide. Similarly, if Canada should be annexed by the United States, Québec would be unable to survive as an isolated island surrounded by an English-speaking American sea. Québecers are intelligent people who will discern, once again, where their true interests lie. Together we can build a strong, progressive union that will be the envy of the world.

WE CAN BOAST A NUMBER OF UNIQUE "FIRSTS"

Canadians should be extremely proud of a number of "firsts" we have contributed. The first rotary snow-blower; the hydrofoil boat; the variable pitch propeller, which made commercial aviation economically viable; the first snowmobile; the first long-distance telephone call; the first transatlantic wireless message; Anik-1, the world's first geostationary domestic communication satellite; the first mobile medical unit; the "cobalt bomb"; the McIntosh apple; pabulum, the Canadian-born baby food; frozen food; the first documentary film; the first commercial motion picture; the first deluxe movie theatre; the paint roller; the green garbage bag,; Superman; and, of course, the Canadarm, now one of the most useful tools in the conquest of space. All of these things, and dozens more, were Canada's contribution to the world scene.

In an effort to encourage young Canadians to learn more about their country, the Canadian Action Party sponsored a "Why Canada is Worth Saving" essay contest in the Spring of 2000. More than 1,600 Canadians, the majority students, expressed their deepest feelings toward their country. Everyone who read some of the entries was deeply moved by what they had to say.

- "Canada is an island of sanity in a world of troubles, and with no one to stand up for it, it could be lost forever."
- "Without Canada, the world is less one tolerant nation."
- "A world without Canada would be a world without hope."
- "It is sad enough that we are being forced to ask ourselves daily, "Will Canada be saved? But is Canada worth saving? Yes, a thousand times!"

The students left no doubt where they stood. They expressed their love for Canada and want to keep it intact and independent.

WE ARE DIFFERENT FROM AMERICANS

One of the most compelling reasons for preserving our independence is that we are different. Our political systems are different. Neither is perfect as recent experience has shown, and both could stand some improvement. But the fact is, for historical reasons, that we have quite profound differences in the way we govern ourselves.

Our style and culture is different from our cousins South of the border. We are the only people in the world who say "excuse me" when someone bumps into us. We eat salmon whereas Americans eat steak. We eat more donuts, too. We are negotiators rather than deal cutters. We consider ourselves as peacekeepers, rather than international policemen. We are nit-pickers, pessimistic and apologetic. Americans believe that in all respects they are the world's greatest.

James J. Blanchard, U. S. Ambassador to Canada from 1993 to 1996, sums up our differences most eloquently. "Canadians have, in most respects, a stronger sense of community, of inter-connectedness, of taking care of each other, of taking time to worry about each other than Americans do. Although in our small towns we still retain that quality. Americans, on the other hand, have a stronger sense of nationhood, of a belief that our best days are ahead, that our history is glorious, that there are values that bind us together, and there's a story about our country we all believe in and are proud of."[10]

We, too, have a history of which we can be proud. We have the additional advantage of being able to enjoy the best of both worlds – the best of globalization and the best from living next door to the U.S., while still preserving those qualities of personality and character that makes us distinct. We are different from Americans – not better, not worse, but different.

And so I say with heart and soul and voice, vive la différence!

POSTSCRIPT

LET'S SAVE CANADA
AND DO OURSELVES AND THE WORLD
A FAVOUR

"It is my dream that this beautiful country will never die."

Pierre Elliot Trudeau

The premise here is that Canada has to be saved, and that it is worth saving. I have tried to make that case in this book realizing, of course, that not everyone agrees. But every poll I have seen, plus my own unofficial sampling, shows that a very large majority want Canada to remain independent. They will be denied their democratic right to choose, however, unless the political scene changes dramatically.

I admit that quite a few have given up. They think that the sell-out has gone so far as to be irreversible. This view is based partly on reality, and partly on the hopelessness of the political situation. The Liberal government is firmly committed to increased integration of the U.S. and Canadian economies, and they don't listen to anyone, including their own dissenting back-benchers. The government's complacency is born of the knowledge that there is no powerful, united political voice opposing them. Even the press, which should be an unofficial opposition, is not. It faithfully backs the globalization line, and contributes to the government's air of infallibility.

So there is no point in even thinking about saving Canada unless there is a new and dynamic political entity firmly committed to standing the status quo on its end. An independent Canada would have to be the centre-piece of its appeal, and it would have to be prepared to abrogate NAFTA, and any other investment treaties that grant national status to foreign investors. These policies would be the foundation on which it would pledge to build a just society for all Canadians.

WHAT CANADA DOES NOT NEED

What Canada does not need is to "unite the right" into one grand conservative party, although you wouldn't get that impression from your daily newspapers, which have been running the story as a serial. The seemingly interminable machinations of the Canadian Alliance as certain of its members, and some of its financial backers, attempted to dump Stockwell Day as leader before the date set by the constitution of the party, was enough to stretch credulity even as a soap opera. It was a dream scene for journalists as they waited for each new exciting chapter until Day finally agreed to an early leadership convention.

How this will affect the push to "unite the right" is not at all clear. There are at least two groups of people involved. There are those who want to win an election, form a government, and enjoy the perks and privileges of office. Another group, of business people, want to construct an alternative to the government that will hold fast to the ideas of continentalism and globalization and not rock the corporate boat. They want a party they can control.

The biggest hurdle is that mixing the Alliance and the Progressive Conservatives is a bit like mixing oil and water. The social conservatives in the Alliance are much too far right for the average Conservative. And some of the Red Tories are too far left for many supporters of the Alliance. They would make frigid bedfellows. So who wants to tango?

The majority of Conservatives are more mainstream, and not too ideological. They have more in common with the

NDP than they do with the Alliance. In fact there has been quite a bit of cross-voting between the two parties over the years that I have been in politics. The big divide between them today is their attitude toward "Free Trade" and globalization. That gulf can only be bridged when PC Leader Joe Clark and his advisers accept the fact that unless Canada does an about-turn, it is doomed. Some of the populist members of the Alliance should come to the same conclusion.

WHAT CANADA NEEDS

What Canadians want and what they need may or may not be identical but they are not contradictory, either. Canadians want a major party that acts and looks like a "government in waiting," an alternative to the governing Liberals. That is what they were looking for at the time of the 2000 election when so many thought that it was time for a change. For a brief moment, some thought the Alliance might fill the bill. Then they took a second look, and decided that right wing politics is incompatible with the hopes and aspirations of the majority – unless that right wing politics happens to be called Liberal.

Canadians also reject left wing politics. They are distrustful of any politics that is perceived as pitting the interests of one class of Canadians against another. It runs contrary to our egalitarian fantasies. Consequently, in the 2000 election, almost half of all Canadians were not sufficiently attracted to any party to bother voting, and that for good reason.

There were too many parties, and too little choice. Not one of the major parties even mentioned the two most important issues facing Canada at the time – that we were losing our country and simultaneously losing our democracy. Too many voters reached the conclusion, correctly, that it didn't matter too much who got in, that nothing of substance was likely to change very much. That reality is Canada's greatest challenge today.

What Canada desperately needs is a broadly based party of the progressive, or slightly radical centre, that is not beholden to either business or labour. By radical, I mean a party willing to make major changes in order to solve seemingly intractable problems – a party that believes in radical surgery rather than just symptom treating. It not only has to appear people-oriented, it must be people-oriented. It must give back to citizens greater control over their own lives and destiny.

The political numbers pretty well dictate the scope of a new party that could achieve these goals. The Liberals have enjoyed about 50% popular support in recent days, and although some of this is directly due to lack of enthusiasm for other parties, it is obvious that a serious challenger would need the backing of almost everyone else. Ideally, then, a new nationalist party would comprise most, if not all, of the Progressive Conservative Party (PC), the New Democratic Party (NDP), the Bloc Quebecois (Bloc), the Canadian Action Party (CAP), the Green Party (Greens), and those populist members of the Alliance whose attachment to Canada is greater than to other, less important, issues. Last, and certainly not least, those Liberals who know and understand what the Chrétien government is doing.

They should know, because Brian Mulroney keeps reminding them. He brags that Chrétien just took his policies of "Free Trade", globalization, the GST, etc. and ran with them. Some do understand, but remain silent in the mistaken hope that a new Liberal leader will change course. Not a chance, as I will explain later, when I return to the subject of Canada's permanent government. Some Liberals are going to have to cut bait if they want to be on the right side of history.

To say that the kind of merger I am proposing is a monumental task is the understatement of the moment. But this is war, and we either have to join forces now or raise the white flag. Speaking personally, I am of the same school as the late New York Yankee slugger, Yogi Berra, who said, "It ain't over 'til it's over." There is still time, but not much time, to put the team together and slay the mighty globalization Goliath.

The obstacles are hubris, self-interest, nostalgia and turf-protection. It will be hard for life-long Conservatives to accept that their party, with its long and illustrious history, is not the party that can evolve as the "government in waiting." But it is clear from the people I talk to, that such a prospect is an impossible dream. Brian Mulroney destroyed the party, and his current effort to help his old adversary, Joe Clark, resurrect it on behalf of his international business friends just won't wash with the Canadian people. Still, the flurry of renewed activity has been sufficient to rekindle Clark's ambition, and this could be an obstacle to progress.

The PC Party is clearly at a crossroad. It can move to the right, and compromise its most important principles, it can continue on its own and suffer a fate not too different from that of the British Liberal Party, or it can reinvent itself as part of something bigger, better, and totally relevant to Canada's needs in the early years of the 21st century.

This latter course should appeal to David Orchard, the runner-up to Joe Clark at the last PC leadership convention. Orchard clings to the fantasy of replacing Clark as leader, and then remaking the PC Party in the image of Sir John A. Macdonald and Sir Robert Borden. My Tory friends tell me that it isn't going to happen. And even if it did, it would be too late to save Canada. So David's many ardent followers will have to persuade him to let his dreams yield to his principles and join hands in helping to lead the "Save Canada" bandwagon.

The Bloc faces a different dilemma. It has no long tradition to abandon. Its only *raison d'être* has been to promote the dissolution of Canada and the establishment of an independent state of Québec. Its principal problem is that this policy, if it appeared to make sense at one time, is no longer viable. Canada, without Québec, would not survive. Québec, without Canada, would surely die and the French language and culture would soon disappear from the face of North America. Already some Québecers, including some separatists, have come to realize that globalization is now the greatest threat, and they will soon be forced to face the reality that their only hope for survival is as part of the Canadian union.

Québecers will ultimately come to this conclusion and when they do the Bloc would be a natural addition to the new party I propose. They are their own brand of social democrats and would fit nicely into a broad-band party. Meanwhile, there is every reason to believe that they would support a new party of this genre rather than the governing Liberals so it is fair to include their numbers in the total when planning to storm the parliamentary ramparts.

The NDP appear to be the most open to change. Its constituency has been shrinking and it is now looking for ways to re-invent itself in order to broaden its appeal and influence. There is no unanimity, however, as to the reason for the malaise and what the solution should be. Some activists believe that a sharp turn to the left would revitalize the party and bring back some of its more passionate former supporters. It might accomplish that much, but it would also guarantee that the NDP, or its successor under a new name, would be limited to the role of gadfly in Canadian politics.

The NDP played this role with distinction for decades and can claim credit for helping to influence the shape and direction of post-World War II politics. But that role has diminished considerably of recent years and now there are new and quite different mountains to climb. The challenge now is to stop the erosion of the hard-won gains of the post-war years and to prevent the new-right from turning the clock back decades through "Free Trade" and unfettered globalized investment.

This cannot be accomplished from the political sidelines! The government pays lip service to consultation and dialogue knowing full well that it has no intention of changing course. The same game would be played by any new "united right". So if the NDP wants to influence Canada's destiny, and with it the destiny of both organized labour and ordinary citizens, it will have to do it from the inside of a party powerful enough to gain power and take action.

Just imagine how many manufacturing jobs there will be in Canada twenty years from now if NAFTA remains and we sign the FTAA. The same would be true for top jobs in banking, insurance and just about everything else, assuming that the Maple Leaf Flag is still flying – which is not guaranteed. So Canadians of all political stripes are going to have to decide where their priorities lie before the political deck is shuffled and the winning, or losing, hand dealt.

A winning hand is most likely with a three party system which includes the perpetual Liberals, a new "progressive" party which encompasses the hopes and aspirations of the majority of Canadians, and the Alliance, on the right, which can play the role of gadfly. It has a small natural constituency which deserves to be heard and which would not be comfortable in any party more representative of the population as a whole.

It would be hoped that the Green Party would cooperate in the national interest, although it includes hard-liners who might try to hold-out. It would be the responsibility of the rank-and-file members to apply the appropriate pressure if leaders were less than responsive.

THE NEW POLITICS INITIATIVE

Canadians should be grateful to the initiators of the New Politics Initiative (NPI) for opening up the political debate at a critical time in Canada's history. Their Vision Statement sets out what the co-founders imagine for a new progressive party. After reading it I am convinced that many Canadians, perhaps even a majority, would be quite comfortable with eighty or ninety percent of what they propose. So the potential is virtually unlimited, and I think they set their sights far too low when they suggest that it is a vision designed for the left in politics.

The problem is the same old one of presentation and semantics. They speak of capitalism and socialism as if they were monoliths, when in fact they are not. Socialism, as practiced in Eastern Europe, was state capitalism and it proved to be a disaster. Privately administered capital, when it was subject to reasonable restraint by the state, produced much wealth for its owners, employees, and the population at large, through the taxes it paid. When capitalism seeks to escape the restraints of nation states, however, and set its own rules, it evolves into an evil empire every bit as bad, and in respect of the number of people affected, even worse than the evil empire that was the Soviet Union.

Instead of getting hung up on labels such as left and right, it is more productive to concentrate on the issues, individually. When we do, we will find that there are people right across the old political spectrum who have far more goals in common than there are issues that divide them. In the general election of 2000, for example, the Canadian Action Party was perceived by many as being left of the NDP. Yet we didn't think of ourselves that way. We perceived ourselves as representing the progressive, slightly radical centre because we were talking about the essential issues that make or break our country as a caring, compassionate society.

One of the few significant differences that I have with the NPI is their initial position on NAFTA and the WTO, which I quote as follows. "In the short term we can press for abolishing the kangaroo courts of the WTO and NAFTA, dumping NAFTA's infamous Chapter 11, and stopping trade agreements from impinging on the democratic rights of nation states to regulate their economy and resources and provide public services." Ultimately they would negotiate new agreements more to their liking.

The sponsors must know that their proposal is just wishful thinking. It is not "New Politics," it is the same old politics of equivocation and obfuscation. The promise is similar to one Jean Chrétien made before the 1993 general election and then proceeded to ignore. The "kangaroo courts" are an integral part of the treaties and the only way to "abolish" them is to abrogate and get out from under the treaties. I hope, therefore, that the initiators will adjust their policy and adopt a clear-cut and unequivocal position of abrogating NAFTA and withdrawing from the WTO forthwith upon forming a government, in order to restore sovereignty and democracy to the Canadian electorate.

Another area where the stance of the NPI must be sharpened is in the area of monetary and banking reform. It nods gently in this direction by calling for the "Democratization of the Bank of Canada," and mentioning the subject of cash reserves for the private banks. But these are fundamental rather than peripheral issues. It was the banking system, with its inevitable economic booms and busts, which was the genesis of the division between left and right in politics. Owners of capital courted workers when the economy was expanding rapidly, and then dumped them like so many over-ripe cabbages when recession struck. Anyone who really cared about people as individuals was appalled by the inhumanity of the system.

Just as it was the banking aspect of capitalism which created the great divide between capital and labour, it can be the reform which can bridge the gulf between left and right. If half of the new money created each year was government-created money, used on behalf of all of the people who have priority rights to it, many of our seemingly intractable problems could be easily solved.

It would no longer be necessary to pit those people who want to see more money spent to protect the environment, to provide excellent health care, to build social housing, to make public education more universally acceptable and for other worthy purposes against those who want lower tax rates and orderly debt reduction. A well run economy can easily accommodate both.

This is particularly important as we head into a period when the need for infrastructure is so phenomenal. Estimates of the cost of bringing water purification systems up to standard run in the billions. The same is true of other essential municipal services including sewers, roads and public transportation. The list extends to provincial and federal projects including billions for roads, affordable housing, provincial and national parks and historic sites and monuments.

While I was writing this chapter I heard a news broadcast to the effect that old Fort Henry, in Kingston, is in need of $38 million in reparations with the federal and provincial governments arguing, as usual, about whose responsibility it is to pay. Torontonians, whether they lament or rejoice over the decision for the 2008 Olympics, hope that the city will not be neglected and that the billions required for waterfront development, replacing the Gardiner Expressway, and improving the public transportation system can be found. Unless it can be found, Toronto's place in the international urban firmament will continue to decline. Other cities have comparable needs.

Very large sums of debt free, and low cost (say 3%) money are absolutely essential to the bright and shining future that everyone, both left and right, would like to see. Without it, there will be constant wrangles between levels of governments, which are getting extremely tedious for impatient souls who want to see things done, and between left and right with one wanting governments to build the waterworks, roads and sewers, and the other which will advocate private, for profit, development which will obfuscate both the long-term real cost and ultimate responsibility to users and taxpayers. For anyone who wants to see governments remain responsible and accountable, monetary reform is the only road to take.

THE PERMANENT GOVERNMENT

The NPI Vision Statement raises one question of absolutely fundamental importance which needs to be fully aired and addressed. It states: "As too many NDP provincial governments have found to their chagrin, you don't 'win power' simply by 'winning an election.'" This truism applies not just to NDP governments, it applies to all governments. Remember that Brian Mulroney got elected by promising "jobs, jobs, jobs," and didn't deliver. Then Jean Chrétien got elected by promising "jobs, jobs, jobs," and didn't deliver. In both cases their good intentions were frustrated by the overwhelming power of the Canadian permanent government, which is similar in kind, if not in scope, with the American permanent government.

Our permanent government is comprised of the hundred largest corporations, the big legal firms that do their work, the big public relations and major lobbying firms that work on both public opinion and government opinion, and the top mandarins both civil and military. One significant difference between our establishment and the one south of the border is in the military.

The Pentagon wields enormous power – far too much for the public good, not to mention world peace. The Canadian military is essentially toothless, although a top Air Force officer spoke out on behalf of Canada supporting the U.S. National Missile Defense. Also, you can be almost certain that every time Defence Minister Art Eggleton says anything about his department it was written for him by the senior officers. Still, the military influence is minimal.

Big business exercises its clout both directly, through access to the Prime Minister, Finance Minister Paul Martin and other key ministers, and through the Business Council on National Issues (BCNI) which is one of the most powerful organizations in the country. The BCNI actively promoted the FTA and raised millions of dollars for advertising designed to influence public opinion.

It was no small coincidence that some months before the general election of 1993, the BCNI picked four opposition MPs, who were likely candidates for cabinet in the event of a Liberal victory, to wine and dine over a menu of business concerns. It is equally no small coincidence that the four became strong right wing ministers pushing issues like the extension of "free trade" and globalization.

The disproportionate influence exercised by big business cannot be discussed without getting into the area of election finance. In most Western democracies, governments, and "governments-in-waiting," are "bought" by big business. To restore any semblance of genuine democracy, strict limits will have to be applied to both the size of donations, and the amount of money that can be spent on advertising.

I have suggested that a new party might limit donations from any business, union local, or individual to $10,000 annually. I don't think any party can be "bought" for that sum. Once in office, it could change the Elections Act and reduce that amount to $5,000. That would create a much more level playing field, and no party would have to be beholden to vested interests of either the right or the left. I don't really believe that either the lower sum or the "contributions from individuals only" approach is realistic for a party attempting to defeat a government with overwhelming financial backing.

While the power and influence of big business cannot be underestimated, it is the top mandarins who call the shots, in the majority of cases. They are usually bright, dedicated people with considerable experience to support their views, and Canada can be justly proud of the quality of their contribution to Canadian and international public life over the years.

The problem is that tenure and long-service can lead to a sense of superior wisdom and proprietorship. They think they own the country and know best how to govern it. Many readers will have seen the British sitcom, "Yes Minister". The reason it was so funny was because it was so close to real life. Senior officials develop a knack for influencing the opinions of politicians and getting them to adopt the establishment position as their own. Sometimes the politicians convince themselves that the ideas originate with them. In truth, the top mandarins are just as fallible as the rest of us. Some personal experiences will help to explain my skepticism.

It was always the dream of people who lived in Ottawa that the Rideau Canal be flooded and used as a skating rink in winter. At least two official reports concluded that it was impossible. Finally, a Chairman of the National Capital Commission, Douglas Fullerton, who didn't understand the meaning of the word impossible, directed that it be done anyway. Now, as everyone knows, "the longest skating rink in the world" is one of the National Capital's principal winter attractions enjoyed by thousands of residents and visitors alike.

Two somewhat extreme examples occurred during my time in the Trudeau government. In the Fall of 1968, at a time when Central (later Canada) Mortgage and Housing Corporation was part of my responsibility, there was a shortage of money for mortgages to finish out the season. I asked the cabinet for more, knowing pretty well in advance what the response would be. There was no money available. Still, the need was urgent, and I put forward a compromise proposal. I asked for permission to sell $68 million of mortgages from the Corporation's portfolio and invest the money in new housing.

It was a reasonable compromise so the Minister of Finance, Ben Benson agreed, and cabinet approved. Early the following morning I got a call from Bob Bryce, the Deputy Minister of Finance. "Paul," he said, "no deal." "But cabinet approved," I replied. "No deal" he responded. "Your minister was there, and he agreed," I continued. "Dammit," Bob exclaimed, "I don't care what the minister said, there is no deal!" That was the end of it.

Thirty years later, when I read cabinet minutes in the course of writing my memoirs, I found that all reference to the decision had been expunged. It simply said that the minister of finance and the minister of transport would have further discussions concerning money for mortgages. The old boys net was so powerful that even cabinet minutes could be doctored to suit the occasion.

It was the same establishment group that put the knife in my back as a result of the Task Force on Housing and Urban Development. They claimed that I had compromised cabinet authority by acting as chairman of the Task Force, and asked me to fudge the books and deny that I had been chairman – this after I had been on television three or four nights a week for several months clearly identified as chairman. I don't fudge books, which made me quite unpopular in high places.

That, however, was not their real complaint. I had taken the new prime minister at his word when he talked about participatory democracy. So the Task Force had listened to the experts during the day, and then held Town Hall meetings at night to listen to the people, even though the experts said they were not competent to speak for themselves. My colleagues and I found them extremely articulate, and quite capable of expressing their opinions which were about

180 degrees opposite from those of the experts. We concluded that the people knew what they were talking about and incorporated many of their suggestions in the report.

That was the problem. Implementing some of the ideas would have cut into the turf of the Ottawa establishment, so they put the heat on the PM. He was still new to the job, and not as secure as he later became, so he sided with the bureaucrats, even though he was aware that I understood the subject better than the officials. That left me with the unhappy choice of either compromising my principles or resigning, and I chose the latter.

Some time after my departure, Gordon Robertson, who was clerk of the privy council at the time of my ordeal, addressed students at Carleton University. Somehow my name came up in the course of the question period. "The problem with Hellyer," he said, "was that he thought politicians were elected to come to Ottawa and make policy." Robertson had me figured out correctly. Would anyone want to run for office just to be a rubber stamp for the bureaucrats?

This brings me back to the nature of the problem. In my opinion, about twenty-five or thirty men and women, mostly men, have wrecked Canada in the last two decades by giving the governments of the day bad advice. The three epicentres of disaster have been the Bank of Canada, the Department of Finance and the Department of Trade. While the first two have undermined the financial viability of the country, it is the conclave of zealots in trade who have been systematically grooming the country for sale. Each successive "loaded" report, be it in telecommunications or transportation, provides a fresh invitation to tear down the border.

I should underline that this is not being done in malice. Most of the insiders will be appalled to hear themselves described as I have pictured them. But they are ideologues, and know not what they do! So any new party, if it wants to implement any new controversial policies, will have to screen and fire some of the more obtuse senior officials in Ottawa.

It won't be necessary to replace them all because the senior ranks of the public service have proliferated in the same way that the number of generals and admirals has grown out of all proportion to the number of troops under command in the Armed Forces. A few new top notch people will be necessary, however, to turn the ship of state around, and head it for safe haven. Without some new people nothing of import will happen.

A NEW BEGINNING

What I am pleading for is a new party comprising several of the existing political parties, and concerned Canadians from all of them, including the governing Liberals. There are members of that party who are willing to put Canada first, if they have the opportunity. The new party's tilt would be toward a caring and compassionate society with equality of opportunity for all. It would be progressive and daring, willing to take risks and back new ideas for the benefit of Canadians and others. It would be a federal party only, so it could cooperate fully, and even-handedly, with provincial governments of any political stripe.

It would be internationally oriented rather than protectionist, but it would pursue agreements based on fair rather than free trade, in order to preserve some capacity to paddle our own canoe. It would support those measures necessary to keep "The True North Strong and Free" both strong, and independent.

It would not be necessary for everyone supporting the formation of such a party to agree on every detailed policy. Everyone has his or her own priorities, and each will be required to make compromises. All that is necessary, at the outset, is a short list of broad principles to assist in the subsequent development of compatible policies. The following list, for discussion purposes only, includes some of the principles many Canadians hold in common.

PRINCIPLES TO CONSIDER

The first and foremost, and the only one that is non-negotiable for me, is the abrogation of NAFTA, and refusal to negotiate or sign the FTAA, in order to get rid of the infamous "national treatment" provision.   A number of Bilateral Investment Treaties (BITs) would also have to be abrogated and replaced with new ones without national treatment.

The following are some other possible commitments:

- A strong, caring and compassionate government.
- Full employment, defined as about 4% unemployed.
- Protection of the environment to rank equally with job creation.
- Encouragement of innovation and entrepreneurship.
- Universal access to first-class health care.
- Universal access to public education.
- Maintenance of public ownership and operation of essential services, including sewers, water and roads.
- Provision of tens of thousands of new units of quality non-profit housing.
- The use of the Bank of Canada to help finance essential services.
- Strong support for the arts and the CBC.
- Providing the Armed Forces with the personnel and equipment necessary to fulfill their assigned tasks.
- Working with First Nations and aboriginal peoples to determine what they want rather than continue the top down approach.
- Parliamentary and electoral reform including proportional representation, limitations on financial contributions, curbs on the prime minister's near-dictatorial power, and an elected Senate.
- The pursuit of an independent foreign policy appropriate to Canadian ideals.

A MESSAGE OF HOPE

Anyone who has read my books, or heard one of my lectures, will know that no matter how pessimistic they may sound, I always conclude with a message of hope. I don't like people telling me how bad things are without providing a clue as to what might be done about it. So I never do. I say that there is at least one solution to every problem, and go on to suggest what I think the preferred one might be.

I began by saying that we were going to lose our country unless we do something about it. That is my conviction. But we can still do something if we are willing to sublimate our own personal interests and prejudices in the interest of the greater good. I have absolutely no doubt that we can save Canada. I have absolutely no doubt that it would be in our own best interest to do so. Our children and grandchildren deserve the same choice that we had. So we would be robbing them of their heritage if we refused to act.

Most young people are idealists. They want to see the kind of unlimited opportunity that we know to be possible. But they want it for all the people of the world as well as themselves. Just think what would be possible on the world scene if a future Canadian government went to a meeting of the G8 and actually proposed that the IMF be wound up, the World Bank converted to an aid agency, the WTO disbanded while new and fairer trading arrangements were devised, and that Third World debt be paid off by increasing cash reserve requirements for the banks.

The effect would be electric. Instead of throwing rocks and bottles at the police, protesters would be waving Canadian flags and urging other world leaders to take note of what ordinary people really hope and pray for. Canada could lead the way. Canada should lead the way because we did the world a great disservice in agreeing to national treatment. In that case we used our power badly. We now have the opportunity to make amends. First we can save Canada, and then go on to achieve great things for ourselves, and for the world.

Chapter 1: Goodbye Canada

1. As reported in the *Toronto Star*, October 22, 1987, in an article "More signs the U.S. believes it beat Canada." Yeutter denied making the statement but *Star* reporter Bob Hepburn added: "However, the U.S. sources, who asked not to be named, are considered impeccable. They were heavily involved in the talks, are extremely close to U.S. Treasury Secretary James Baker and were privy to confidential conversations and documents." I believe that Yeutter did, in fact, make the statement because it sounds like him and what he said would have been what any forward-thinking U.S. negotiator would have thought and said privately when they were not expecting to be reported.
2. Based on Michael B. Smith's recollection of the meeting aboard Smith's 34-foot Sabre Sloop, *Wind*, as recorded in *Building a Partnership: The Canada-United States Free Trade Agreement*, Mordechai Kreinin(ed.). East Lansing: Michigan State University Press, 2001, p. 7.
3. Extrapolated from Industry Canada – Investment Review, March 26, 2001.
4. As reported in the *Vancouver Sun*, January 12, 2000.
5. As reported in the *National Post*, March 2, 2000.
6. Statistics Canada, Fourth Quarter, 2000.
7. *Ibid.*
8. Beauchesne, Eric, "Lame buck better than NAFTA: study", *Ottawa Citizen*, June 20, 2001.
9. Canadian Trade Review, Department of Foreign Affairs and International Trade, Third Quarter, 2000.
10. As reported in the *Globe and Mail*, May 14, 2001.
11. *Ibid.*
12. Dungan, P. and S. Murphy, "The Changing Industry and Skill Mix of Canada's International Trade", *Perspectives on North American Free Trade*, Paper No. 4, Industry Canada, 1999.
13. Campbell, Bruce, "False Promise: Canada in the Free Trade Era, EPI Briefing Paper, April 2001.
14. William McBrien took over as TTC commissioner in 1930 and was elevated to chairman in 1933. He stayed in office for 21 years and literally died in office just weeks after he gave an address at the opening of the Yonge subway on March 30, 1954.
15. Paul Hellyer speaking on the Federal Budget, May 10, 1955.
16. Ray Bassett, of Victoria, BC, former Vice-President of Victoria & Grey Trust, is one who always mentions the incident when he sees

me. (Statistics courtesy of Canada Mortgage and Housing Corporation.)

17. Hon. Willard Z. Estey, Partner at McCarthy Tétrault..

18. Toulin, Alan, "Canada is sliding to ruin: Royal Bank", *National Post*, February 18, 2000.

19. Rubin, Sandra and Robert Thompson, "Canada risks being satellite of multinationals", *National Post*, April 26, 2000.

20. Newman, Peter C., "The End of Canada? Measures to expand free trade will inevitably lead to the end of first our dollar – and then our sovereignty", *Maclean's* , January 8, 2001.

21. Pearlstein, Steven, "O Canada! A National Swan Song?", *Washington Post*, September 5, 2000.

22. Gillis, Charlie, "World's Longest Undefended Border is Quickly Vanishing," *National Post*, September 6, 2000.

23. Editorial, "The 51St state? Never", *National Post*, September 7, 2000.

24. As reported in the *National Post*, June 4, 2001.

Chapter 2: The New World (Dis)Order

1. A report leaked from the 1991 meeting of the Bilderbergers held in Baden-Baden, Germany.

2. Memorandum E-A10, 19 October 1940, CFR, War-Peace Studies, Baldwin Papers, Box 117.

3. Memorandum E-A17, 14 June 1941, CFR, War-Peace Studies, Hoover Library on War, Revolution and Peace.

4. Memorandum T-A25, 20 May, 1942, CFR, War-Peace Studies, Hoover Library on War, Revolution and Peace.

5. *Ibid*.

6. Retinger, J.H., the European Continent, London's Hodge, 1946,

7. New York University Press, 1975.

8. Sklar, Holly (ed.), *Trilateralism: The Trilateral Commission and Elite Planning for World Management*. Boston: South End Press, 1980.

9. *Ibid*.

10. MacArthur, John R., *The Selling of "Free Trade": NAFTA, Washington, and the Subversion of American Democracy*. New York: Hill and Wang, 2000.

11. George, Susan, "Winning the War of Ideas: Lessons from the Gramscian Right", originally published in *Dissent*, Summer 1997.

12. *Ibid*.

13. In an e-mail dated May 2, 2001, from the Montreal Economic Institute and signed by Patrick Leblanc.

14. George, Susan, "Winning the War of Ideas: Lessons from the Gramscian Right", op cit. For the full text and updates, go to www.tni.org/george/articles/dissent.htm

Chapter 3: A Means to the End

1. Kreinin, Mordechai (ed.), *Building a Partnership: The Canada-United States Free Trade Agreement.* East Lansing: Michigan State University Press, 2000.
2. As reported in the *Globe and Mail*, November 25, 1998.
3. Ibid.
4. "The Metalclad Case", update prepared by Michelle Sforza, Public Citizen's Global Trade Watch.
5. Dobbin, Murray, "Water: Right or Commodity?" article in the *National Post*, Financial Post section, February 8, 2001.
6. Westell, Anthony, "Who elected the summit protesters," *Globe and Mail*, March 16, 2001.

Chapter 4: The Enforcers

1. Stevenson, Merril, "A Game of Skill as Well: Survey of International Banking", *The Economist*, March 21, 1987.
2. Solomon, Steven, *The Confidence Game: How Unelected Central Bankers Are Governing the Changed World Economy.* New York: Simon & Schuster, 1995.
3. Chossudovsky, Michel, *The Globalisation of Poverty: Impacts of IMF and World Bank Reforms.* Penang: Third World Network, 1997.
4. Danaher, Kevin (ed.), *50 Years is Enough: The Case Against the World Bank and the International Monetary Fund.* Boston: South End Press, 1994.
5. As reported in the *Globe and Mail*, May 6, 1998.
6. Kapur, Devesh, Lewis, John P., and Webb, Richard, *The World Bank: Its First Half Century.* Washington: Brookings Institution, 1997.
7. Caufield, Catherine, *Masters of Illusion: The World Bank and the Poverty of Nations.* New York: Henry Holt and Company, Inc., 1996.
8. Pearson, Lester B., "Partners in Development", 1969.
9. Bello, Walden, "Global Economic Counterrevolution: How Northern Economic Warfare Devastates the South", in *50 Years is Enough: The Case Against the World Bank and the International Monetary Fund*, Kevin Danaher (ed.). Boston: South End Press, 1994, p. 16.
10. *Ibid.*, p. 17.

11. *Ibid.*, p. 18.
12. *Ibid.*
13. Shiva, Vandana, "International Institutions Practicing Environmental Double Standards", in *50 Years is Enough: The Case Against the World Bank and the International Monetary Fund*, Kevin Danaher (ed.). Boston: South End Press, 1994, pp. 102-103.

Chapter 5: The Death of Democracy

1. Quoted in "Cakes and Caviar: the Dunkel Draft and Third World Agriculture", *Ecologist*, Vol. 23, No. 6, Nov-Dec 1993.
2. Bello, Walden, "Why Reform of the WTO is the Wrong Agenda", 2000.
3. Scoffield, Heather, "Canada to take offensive at WTO talks", *Globe and Mail*, August 20, 1999.
4. Scoffield, Heather, "WTO secretary-general defends organization", *Globe and Mail*, June 5, 2000.
5. Laidlaw, Stuart, "EU beef dispute nears solution", *Toronto Star*, November 10, 1999.
6. Source: The World Trade Organization, from their internet page describing the GATS.
   www.wto.org/wto/services/services.htm
7. Bello, Walden, "Why Reform of the WTO is the Wrong Agenda", 2000.

Chapter 6: The Root of all Evil

1. Galbraith, John Kenneth, *Money, Whence it Came, Where it Went*. Boston: Houghton Mifflin Company, 1975, p. 18.
2. Paul Godfrey, Interview in his office, 333 King St. E., Toronto, December 6, 1994.
3. Peter Cook, Lunch at the Ontario Club, November 2, 1994.
4. William Thorsell, At afternoon tea in his office at the Globe and Mail, December 7, 1994.
5. Diane Francis, Interview at lunch at the Ontario Club, October 28, 1994.
6. See Astle, David, *The Babylonian Woe*. Toronto: Published as a private edition by the author, 1975.
7. Chaffers, William, *Gilda Aurifabrorum: A History of English Goldsmiths and Plateworkers, and Their Marks Stamped on Plate*. London: Reeves & Turner, [1800], p. 210.
8. *Ibid.*

9. Hixson, William F., *Triumph of the Bankers: Money and Banking in the Eighteenth and Nineteenth Centuries*. Westport: Praeger Publishers, 1993, p. 46.
10. Friedman, Milton, *A Program for Monetary Stability*. New York: Fordham University Press, 1959.
11. Lester, Richard A., "Currency Issues to Overcome Depressions in Pennsylvania, 1723 and 1729", *The Journal of Political Economy*, Vol. 46, June 1938, p. 326.
12. Hixson, William F., *Triumph of the Bankers*, op. cit., p. 46.
13. Lester, Richard A., "Currency Issues to Overcome Depressions in Pennsylvania, 1723 and 1729", op. cit., p. 338.
14. *Ibid.*, p. 341
15. Smith, Adam, *Wealth of Nations*. New York: P.F. Collier and Son, 1909, p. 266.
16. Nettles, Curtis P., *The Money Supply of the American Colonies before 1720*. New York: Augustus M. Kelley, 1964, p. 265.
17. Ferguson, E. James, *The Power of the Purse: A History of American Public Finance, 1776-1790*. Chapel Hill: University of North Carolina Press, 1961, p. 16.
18. Hixson, William F., *Triumph of the Bankers*, op. cit., p. 81.
19. Nicolay, John G., and Hay, John (eds.) *Abraham Lincoln: Complete Works*. New York: the Century Co., 1907, 2: p. 264.
20. Angell, Norman, *The Story of Money*. New York: Frederick A. Stokes Co., 1929, p. 294.
21. Grubiak, Olive and Grubiak, Jan, *The Guernsey Experiment*. Hawthorne: Omni Publications, p. 7.
22. *The Public Good: Lessons for the 3rd Millennium*, A Conference in honour of Hon. Allan J. MacEachen, St. Francis Xavier University, Antigonish, Nova Scotia, Canada, July 4-6, 1996.
23. Edison, Thomas, American Inventor (Feb. 11, 1947-Oct. 18, 1931).

Chapter 7: Capitalist Totalitarianism

1. Korten, David, "Democracy for Sale", extract of David Korten's Schumacher Lecture in Bristol on October 17, 1998.
2. FED Chairman Alan Greenspan, in an address to the Annual Convention of the American Society of Newspaper Editors, Washington, April 2, 1998.
3. MacKinnon, Mark, "Canada seeks review of NAFTA's Chapter 11", *Globe and Mail*, December 13, 2000.
4. As reported in the *Ottawa Citizen*, April 24, 2001.
5. The average of five years 1995-1999, International Energy Annual, Dept. of Energy.

6. Drohan, Madelaine, "Central bank safe in Dodge's hands", *Globe and Mail*, December 21, 2000.
7. Editorial, *Globe and Mail*, December 21, 2000.
8. World Bank, Global Development Finance, 1999.
9. *Ibid.*

Chapter 8: Winners and Losers

1. Sir Josiah Stamp, later Baron Stamp, was a director of the Bank of England from 1928-1941.
2. Charles Caccia, former federal Liberal Minister of the Environment, in a CBC radio interview.
3. Scott, Robert E., "NAFTA's Hidden Costs: Trade agreement results in job losses, growing inequality, and wage suppression for the United States", Economic Policy Institute, Briefing Paper, April 2001.
4. Michel, Lawrence, Bernstein, Jared, and John Schmitt, "State of Working America 2001-01, Economic Policy Institute Book." Ithica: ILR Press, an imprint of Cornell University Press, 2001, p. 169.
5. Tonelson, Alan, *Race to the Bottom*. New York: Westview Press, 2001, p. 47.
6. Bronfenbrenner, Kate, "Uneasy terrain: the impact of capital mobility on workers, wages, and union organizing. Commissioned research paper for the U.S. Trade Deficit Review Commission, 2000.
7. *Ibid.*
8. Source: Redway and Butler, Barristers & Solicitors, July 22, 1999.
9. As reported in the *Globe and Mail*, July 2, 1997.
10. *Ibid.*
11. As related by Robert Evans, former President of Penmans Ltd., a wholly owned subsidiary of Dominion Textiles.

Chapter 9: Economics 2001

1. Friedman, Milton and Friedman, Rose, *Free to Choose: A Personal Statement*. New York: Harcourt Brace Jovanovich, Inc., 1981.
2. Weintraub, Sidney, *Capitalism's Inflation and Unemployment Crisis: Beyond Monetarism and Keynesiasm.* New York: Addison-Wesley Publishing Co. Inc., 1978.
3. Friedman, Milton and Friedman, Rose, *Free to Choose: A Personal Statement*, op. cit.

4. *Annual Report of the Council of Economic Advisers*, Washington, D.C., January 1979, p. 82.
5. The table showing data for 15 OECD countries can be found in other books by Paul Hellyer including *Surviving the Global Financial Crisis: The Economics of Hope for Generation X.*
6. McCarthy, W.E.J., O'Brien, J.F., and V.G. Dowd, *Wage Inflation and Wage Leadership: A Study of the Role of Key Wage Bargains in the Irish System of Collective Bargaining.* Dublin: Cahill & Co. Ltd., 1975.
7. As reported in the *National Post,* March 12, 2001.
8. Hellyer, Paul, In a keynote address to the Young Liberals of Canada, Banff, Alberta, 1961.
9. Hellyer, Paul, *Agenda: A Plan for Action.* Toronto: Prentice-Hall of Canada Ltd., 1971.
10. Hellyer, Paul, *Exit Inflation.* Toronto: Nelson Canada Limited, 1981.
11. This figure was calculated by assuming that the combined federal and provincial debt would remain at the 1980 level and that the interest payable each year would remain constant at the 1980 figure annually.
12. Statistics Canada and Bank of Canada.
13. Australian Economic Statistics 1949/50 – 1994/95. Published by the Reserve Bank of Australia, Occasional Paper 8, 1996.
14. Departments of the Treasury and Labor.
15. Federal Reserve Board
16. As reported in the *Wall Street Journal.*
17. Watson, William, in the *National Post.*
18. As reported in the *Globe and Mail,* March 23, 2001.
19. As reported in the *Globe and Mail,* May 8, 2001.
20. *Ibid.*
21. *Ibid.*

Chapter 10: A Better Vision

1. Stiglitz, Joseph, in *The New Republic,* April 17, 2000.
2. Adams, Patricia, "The Doctrine of Odious Debts", Interview by Juliette Majot, in *50 Years is Enough: the Case Against the World Bank and the International Monetary Fund*, Kevin Danaher (ed.), Boston: South End Press, 1994, p. 36.
3. King, Dr. Martin Luther Jr., (January 16, 1929 – April 4, 1968).

Chapter 11: Mister President

1. George W. Bush, "A friend is someone who is willing to tell the truth." At a press conference announcing the U.S. was backing out of the Kyoto Protocol, March 29, 2001.
2. As reported in the *Toronto Star*, May 1, 2001.
3. Lapham, Lewis, "Pax Iconomica", in *Behind the Headlines*, Vol. 54, No. 2, Winter 1996-97, p. 9, in his 'On Politics, Culture and Media' keynote address to the Canadian Institute of International Affairs national foreign policy conference in October, 1996.
4. *Ibid.*, p. 8.
5. As reported in the *Toronto Star*, October 22, 1998.
6. As reported in the *Toronto Star*, May 4, 1998.
7. As reported in the *New York Times*, September 3, 1998.
8. As reported in the *Globe and Mail*, March 12, 2001.
9. President George W. Bush's Inaugural Address, January 20, 2001.
10. As reported in the *Toronto Star*, May 10, 2001.
11. President George W. Bush's Inaugural Address, op. cit.
12. *Ibid.*
13. As reported in the *National Post*, June 30, 2001

Chapter 12: Vive la différence

1. Fax to Rt. Hon. Brian Mulroney, May 9, 2001.
2. From an interview with Donald S. Macdonald in his office, June 7, 2001.
3. The State of the Nation, Quarterly Report, Edition One, June 2001.
4. "A Trade Policy That Works for Canada" in Creating Opportunity: The Liberal Plan for Canada, 1993, p. 23.
5. *Ibid.*, p. 24.
6. Tomlin, Alan, "Union with U.S. on Table", *National Post*, June 29, 2001.
7. *Ibid.*,
8. *Ibid.*,
9. "Yugoslavia: The Avoidable War, Co-produced by George Bogdanich and German TV producer Martin Mettmayer. New York International Independent Film & Video Festival Award, Best Social Documentary, September 1999.
10. Blanchard, James, "An Ambassadorial View, in *Building a Partnership: The Canada-United States Free Trade Agreement*, Mordechai Kreinin, (ed.), East Lansing, Michigan State University Press, 2001, p. 125

BIBLIOGRAPHY

Angell, Norman, *The Story of Money*, New York: Frederick A. Stokes Co., 1929.

Astle, David, *The Babylonian Woe*, Toronto: Published as a private edition by the author, 1975.

Bello, Walden, "Global Economic Counterrevolution: How Northern Economic Warfare Devastates the South", in *50 Years is Enough: The Case Against the World Bank and the Inter-National Monetary Fund*, Kevin Danaher (ed.), Boston: South End Press, 1994.

Caufield, Catherine, *Masters of Illusion: The World Bank and the Poverty of Nations*, New York: Henry Holt and Company, Inc., 1996.

Chaffers, William, *Gilda Aurifabrorum: A History of English Goldsmiths and Plateworkers, and Their Marks Stamped on Plate*, London: Reeves & Turner, [1800].

Chossudovsky, Michel, *The Globalisation of Poverty: Impacts of IMF and World Bank Reforms*, Penang: Third World Network, 1997.

Danaher, Kevin (ed.), *50 Years is Enough: The Case Against the World Bank and the International Monetary Fund*, Boston: South End Press, 1994.

De Soto, Hernando, *"The Mystery of Capital: Why Capitalism is Failing Outside the West and Why the Key to Its Success is Right Under Our Noses*, Boulder: Basic Books, 2000.

Ferguson, E. James, *The Power of the Purse: A History of American Public Finance, 1776-1790*, Chapel Hill: University of North Carolina Press, 1961.

Friedman, Milton and Friedman, Rose, *Free to Choose: A Personal Statement*. New York: Harcourt Brace Jovanovich, Inc.,1981.

Friedman, Milton, *A Program for Monetary Stability*, New York: Fordham University Press, 1959.

Galbraith, John Kenneth, *Money, Whence it Came, Where it Went*, Boston: Houghton Mifflin Company, 1975.

Hellyer, Paul, *Exit Inflation*, Toronto: Nelson Canada Limited, 1981.

Hellyer, Paul, *Agenda: A Plan for Action*, Toronto: Prentice-Hall of Canada Ltd., 1971.

Hixson, William F., *Triumph of the Bankers: Money and Banking in the Eighteenth and Nineteenth Centuries*, Westport: Praeger Publishers, 1993.

Kapur, Devesh, Lewis, John P., and Webb, Richard, *The World Bank: Its First Half Century*, Washington: Brookings Institution, 1997.

Kreinin, Mordechai (ed.), *Building a Partnership: The Canada-United States Free Trade Agreement*, East Lansing: Michigan State University Press, 2000.

Nettles, Curtis P., *The Money Supply of the American Colonies before 1720*, New York: Augustus M. Kelley, 1964, p. 265.

Nicolay, John G., and Hay, John (eds.) *Abraham Lincoln: Complete Works*, New York: the Century Co., 1907.

MacArthur, John R., *The Selling of "Free Trade": NAFTA, Washington, and the Subversion of American Democracy*, New York: Hill and Wang, 2000.

McCarthy, W.E.J., O'Brien, J.F., and V.G. Dowd, *Wage Inflation and Wage Leadership: A Study of the Role of Key Wage Bargains in the Irish System of Collective Bargaining*. Dublin: Cahill & Co. Ltd., 1975.

Nettles, Curtis P., *The Money Supply of the American Colonies before 1720*, New York: Augustus M. Kelley, 1964.

Nicolay, John G., and Hay, John (eds.) *Abraham Lincoln: Complete Works*, New York: the Century Co., 1907, 2: p. 264.

Sklar, Holly (ed.), *Trilateralism: The Trilateral Commission and Elite Planning for World Management*, Boston: South End Press, 1980.

Smith, Adam, *Wealth of Nations*, New York: P.F. Collier and Son, 1909.

Solomon, Steven, *The Confidence Game: How Unelected Central Bankers Are Governing the Changed World Economy*, New York: Simon & Schuster, 1995.

Tonelson, Alan, *Race to the Bottom*, New York: Westview Press, 2001.

Weintraub, Sidney, *Capitalism's Inflation and Unemployment Crisis: Beyond Monetarism and Keynesiasm*. New York: Addison-Wesley Publishing Co. Inc., 1978.

INDEX